CREATING

WEALTH

THROUGH

SELF-STORAGE

The Everyman's Guide to
Self-Storage Success

MARK HELM

ISBN13: 978-1-5055-0519-1
ISBN10: 1505505194

Limits of Liability and Disclaimer of Warranty

The author and publisher shall not be liable for your misuse of this material. This book is strictly for informational and educational purposes.

Warning—Disclaimer

The purpose of this book is to educate and entertain. The author and/or publisher do not guarantee that anyone following these techniques, suggestions, tips, ideas, or strategies will become successful. The author and/or publisher shall have neither liability nor responsibility to anyone with respect to any loss or damage caused, or alleged to be caused, directly or indirectly by the information contained in this book.

Contents

WHO IS MARK HELM?

Mark Helm is a commercial real estate agent who began specializing in self-storage in the mid-1990s. By 2000, he had purchased his first self-storage project. Since then he has had many ups and downs in real estate; and more specifically the self-storage industry. He has made almost every mistake that can be made, and yet, through the mistakes, Mark has developed a system of analyzing and buying self-storage that has a proven track record.

As every entrepreneur discovers, just knowing something does not make the difference. To be truly successful in any endeavor or in life itself, one must confront what is inside them that holds them back. It is a continual process of breaking oneself up and reforming in such a manner, that what was not possible before is now possible. The struggles Mark faces as he grows his self-storage portfolio are addressed in this book in ways that are accessible to the reader.

Mark has a personal goal to build a $60,000,000 self-storage portfolio and is fast approaching it. For him to achieve this goal, a system had to be developed. Through many trials and tribulations, such a system emerged and it is presented in this book. Even the financial analysis software was designed by him because of a lack of it in this industry is made available through this book.

Mark, throughout his real estate career, has had the following highlights:
- Broker/owner of a full service real estate company for 12 years.
- A CCIM (Certified Commercial Industrial Member) designee since the mid-1990s (the highest designation in the commercial real estate industry).

- Number-one commercial real estate agent in his region for six years starting in 1996.

Mark has been married to his wife Rebecca for 25 years, and has three children and four grandchildren. He also plays guitar in a bluegrass band, BlueZenGrass (**www.BlueZenGrass.com**).

To find out more about Mark Helm and/or the services he can provide, visit **www.CreatingWealthThroughSelfStorage.com**.

To the Reader

When I read the first draft of this book, I was shocked at the number of times the word *I* was in the book. Although this is an exploration into my entry into the world of self-storage, it is really about you—the possibility of you finding a niche, creating a dream, and, with no apparent training or resources, creating something much bigger than yourself or anything you could have initially imagined.

For me self-storage is the vehicle. I don't really understand why it isn't for everyone, but I realize it is not. Whatever the vehicle is for you, my hope is this work will assist you and inspire you to listen to what is within, not what people tell you, and take the next step toward fulfilling it.

I specifically intended this work to be for someone who wants to get into the self-storage business (the greatest business on earth!) but, as I wondered: How can a person like me do it? Unlike many startups, one cannot bootstrap (use little or no funds, credit cards, or less) to create a self-storage business. Like most real estate, it cost lots of money and, 99 percent of the time, one needs to leverage their way into the business with debt. I had, like I am assuming most of you have, little money to get in the business. So realistically, how can someone truly get in the business, and create real wealth and cash flow from self-storage (or any real estate asset, really) without lots of money? If I don't have the money, where can I get it?

This book is designed to show you how—or at least how I did it. There it goes again: *I*. Really, it takes a lot more than one person. Throughout this book when you read *I*, know there is an entire community behind the person writing *I*.

The people who will work with me at the facilities are a constant source of inspiration to me. I never cease to be amazed at the ownership people will take if given the opportunity. The managers and others who work at the facilities own them in their minds and hearts. They run them so much better than I ever could, and free me up to play this game of growing the business. Without them, I would spend every moment working *in* the business, not *on* the business. They know the game being played to grow the business and the goals I created, and are the best cheerleaders and source of operational information to fulfill the game possible. I love and appreciate them more than they will ever know. I truly wish I could pay them what they are worth. I strive to have a creative, fun, and self-directed work environment, and hope the efforts in that direction somewhat compensate them for their efforts.

Without my partners, it would be impossible to play and have a chance at winning at this game of creating wealth through self-storage. When the computer crashes, when the gates don't work, when a manager calls in sick—on and on—Maria, my partner who runs the day to day operations of the facilities, is there. I have no doubts she will make sure the customers can get to their units or they pay their bills regardless of what is going on. If I had the sole responsibility for this, believe me, this business would be one or two facilities. My partner's ability to handle the day-to-day operations is astounding and a vital component in any business. Maria especially compensates for many of my weaknesses, and her willingness to put up with all the *I*'s thrown her way by me in daily activity is a testament to her ability to work with anyone. The customers, employees, and her partners truly appreciate her. The partners who go on the loans with me and make it possible for a bank to loan us millions of dollars— well, this is amazing to me. The trust they put in me and in Maria, the managing partner, is so immense it is sometimes hard to believe.

Very few businesses can grow without money, and the people who invest in the projects I present them with are the lifeblood of our growth. I never cease to be amazed that someone really thinks we have a great idea about self-storage and is willing to put their money into our dreams. Their investment money is sacred to me and the partners, and I hope the investors know it. Above all else, their capital makes it possible for the game to be played and it must be protected at all cost. But at times I just shake my head. It is still exciting and thrilling every time someone says "I am in." *I* have a vision and dream, and they get it. It becomes theirs, and we must use every effort to ensure their (our) dream is fulfilled.

And last and most important of all, behind the *I's* in this book, is my family. I sure wouldn't like to have to put up with all the stuff my wife, Rebecca, does with me: the times I am gone, the vacations that always end up with me on the phone, the getting up early every morning and going to bed early so that I have the time and energy to play this game. Of all the people who really have to deal with the *I,* it is Rebecca. She runs the house and creates a loving environment that supports me, all while she has her own career working with veterans in the mental health field, a noble and truly needed job that makes a real difference in the lives of our veterans.

So behind every *I* in this book, remember this team of people that makes it possible for the *I* to write about his love affair with self-storage.

If you have ever wondered how to get into self-storage—or, for that matter, any business that requires money to get in and grow—this is how *I* did it. There will be a lot of resources designed for the person growing a self-storage business available in the book and at **www.CreatingWealthThroughSelfStorage.com**.

This book has a lot of ideas and strategies on the art of finding and acquiring self-storage. However, I get bored with just strategies and ideas. Almost every other chapter title begins with the word *APPLICATION,* and includes true-life examples of how the strategy in the previous chapter looked in real life as we acquired a self-storage facility. And finally, we end with a case study, going from start to finish acquiring a facility showing all the things that worked and that did not work.

My hope is you will create your own world of *I* and self-storage is the vehicle.

CreatingWealthThroughSelfStorage.com

After years of being in the business of acquiring self-storage facilities and developing what many consider the premiere analysis program to determine current value and project future cash flows, Mark now makes this program available to you to use at **www.CreatingWealthThroughSelfStorage.com**.

This website offers a host of tools, tips, and resources for people getting in, or expanding their holdings in the self-storage industry. After 20 years of helping companies large and small, as well as other investors, and building his own company's portfolio, many of his tools are now made available to you.

If you are considering getting into the self-storage business or growing one you already have, this site is for you! Be sure to download the **"Ten Most Made Mistakes"** in the self-storage business for free. Mark also has the financial analysis software he has developed over the years available online. This is the one he personally uses when looking at and buying self-storage facilities. Use the code CWTSS in the discount code space and get $100.00 off the price of the software.

Visit the site, browse, and utilize whatever tools and resources you may need to purchase your next self-storage facility.

Chapter 1
Random Call

"It is easier to act yourself into a new way of feeling rather than feel your way into a new way of acting."
~ **G. D. Morgan**

I am amazed at the seeming randomness of life. One chance phone call, a chance meeting, meeting a person who knows someone, or just bumping into a stranger—all can alter the course of one's entire life.

On a spring morning in May 1995, I happened to be in my commercial real estate office around 10:30 a.m. I had spent the previous four years in classrooms off and on across the country, studying to get what is considered the highest designation in the commercial real estate industry, the CCIM designation. (CCIM is the global leader in commercial and investment real estate education and services, and the CCIM designation, recognized as a hallmark of professional competency, affords members an undisputed competitive advantage). I sure hoped all this work would make a difference and the money to achieve the designation would pay off. I was playing catch up in my commercial real estate practice. Just the week before, I had checked to make sure my name was in the CCIM roster, wondering if this would ever really generate any business for me.

The phone rang that May morning, and thank goodness I happened to be there in the office instead of with a client, or in an office building my company managed, or in the countless other places I usually was. (This was before the proliferation of the use of cell phones). It turned out I was not the first person this individual called off the CCIM roster for our market; I was just the first person to pick up the telephone. The person making the call was the acquisition director for a national self-storage REIT who wanted to enter our market. In the mid-1990s, REITS (real estate investment trusts, or publicly traded or private companies that invest in real estate) were hungry to buy. This particular person I talked to that morning seemed almost panicked. Later, I learned his job depended on the number of acquisitions he successfully closed.

That morning he asked, "Could you help me find self-storage to buy in your market?" Here is a tip: If you ask a real estate agent if they can help you buy real estate, usually there is only one answer.

I had never sold self-storage, but how hard could it be? I knew about office buildings, retail shopping centers, and industrial real estate. I knew how income-producing commercial real estate works from my newly received and hard-won CCIM designation. An appointment was set, and I dove headfirst into the world of self-storage. To this day, I just keep going deeper and deeper.

When I received that phone call, I was listing and selling commercial real estate, and I was a partner in a property management company that leased and managed primarily office buildings in Louisville's central business district. At that point in my career, my major emphasis was on leasing and selling office space and buildings. I had never even thought about self-storage. I basically sold office buildings to a group of investors I knew, managed and re-positioned them in the market (fancy words for refurbishing the buildings, re-leasing them, and increasing the money they generate), then sold them, hopefully for a profit. I lived on the fees and commissions generated from that activity. I was not an owner in anything I managed.

Actually, I was glad not to be an owner in the office buildings I managed. I quickly saw in the type of real estate I was managing, that office buildings can cost a lot of money. The rent I was able to get from the tenants for our clients was good, and we were actually quite adept at keeping operating expenses under control, but the cost to replace a tenant was expensive—very expensive sometimes. Office tenants expect owners to create office space that works for them, which often means tearing walls out, putting new walls up, painting, installing new floors, and on and on. Even if a tenant renews their lease, we had to budget money to repaint or replace carpet. On and on. It cost a lot of money to keep the rent stream going in office buildings.

I cannot tell you the number of times we had to place a dumpster in the alley of the office buildings we were managing back then. We'd have a chute attached from a window, and all the walls and ceilings would come down the chute into the dumpster. Then we would construct a new office plan in that space so the new tenant would move in and start paying rent. And, oh yes, I had to get paid for that as well as the real estate agent who brought the tenant to our building, so there was a commission, too, on top of the tenant "improvement" cost.

Every now and then we could get a prospective tenant to accept the floor plan of a particular vacant space, but we'd still have to paint, install carpet, and do some minor improvements; even tenants who renewed their lease and stayed in place required some painting or new flooring. At that time, our cost of renewals ran about $4.50 to $5.50 per square foot.

Yes, owning commercial real estate seemed very expensive to me. I was glad I was the manager and leasing agent. But I knew I did not want to do that forever. Was I missing it? How could a guy like me, somewhat on the ball but not someone with a lot of money, move from leasing and selling real estate to owning something that created real wealth? It did not appear to be office buildings for me.

Could I Really Do It? My Dream Begins

After I started working and helping the acquisition director for the REIT I mentioned, and will detail in this chapter, I for the first time saw a type of real estate I could own without the drawbacks I saw in owning office buildings or retail buildings. It was clear after owning two houses that I did not want to be in the residential real estate business. First of all, almost everyone who wants to get in the business starts there, so there is a lot of competition. But I quickly saw I did not have the stomach for evicting a family. It kept me up at night.

I was struggling making a living by listing, selling, and leasing commercial real estate, and for the first time I saw the possibility that I could own self-storage for the reasons listed later in this chapter. Self-storage has some real benefits other commercial income-producing real estate does not have. But me—could I actually move from selling self-storage to owning it? Was it possible? Really?

Could I move from having to earn my income from my labor to owning a type of real estate that creates income 24 hours a day and goes up in value every year, creating wealth for me? Self-storage has great income potential and low overhead. I had never seen anything with a lower cost to own than self-storage. It is amazing. You will see through this book the real advantages that self-storage offers. If you are not in love with it now, you soon will be.

Perhaps I was ready, but by the mid-1990s I had been in the real estate business 10 years and was wondering if this was all there was for me. Don't get me wrong: listing and selling commercial real estate is an interesting business, but the income swings were tremendous. I was helping others create wealth; when was I going to do the same for myself? Also, if I was not working, there was no money.

If anyone wants to create wealth through real estate, especially self-storage, there are a few terms and concepts one needs to know. Here is a quick crash course in income-producing real estate.

Income-Producing Real Estate

All income-producing real estate is valued by taking the gross income the property generates (rent), less the operating expenses (taxes, maintenance, utilities, insurance, etc.). That number is called net operating income (NOI). Theoretically, the rate of return a ready, willing, and able buyer is willing to pay for that income stream (capitalization rate, or CAP rate) determines the value of the asset. As an example, take two different income-producing properties: (1) a low-income, tax credit housing property, and (2) a "Triple Net

Leased" (NNN) retail building with an AAA-rated public company as the tenant. (NNN means the tenant pays all the expenses including taxes and insurance, making the rent the NOI for the owner). In this example, both properties generate a $100,000 NOI. The market CAP rate for the NNN property (i.e., what ready, willing, and able buyers are willing to pay for that $100,000 income stream) is 7%. In other words, for a relatively hassle-free, relatively safe income stream, the market is willing to pay someone a price that would generate a 7% return (calculated by dividing $100,000 by .07). That places a value of $1,428,571 for that $100,000 income stream if the income is generated by a NNN retail building with an AAA-rated public company as the tenant.

The low-income tax credit example, which has more risk, more management issues to deal with, and a less secure income stream, may require a higher rate of return by the market. A property of that type may command a 12% return (CAP rate). Therefore the value of that asset would be $833,333 ($100,000 divided by .12). Same $100,000 NOI, but the CAP rate used will determine the value.

Another factor in determining the ultimate rate of return for an investor is the expenses beyond operating expenses that are "below" the net operating income line. These are usually debt service (the loan payments), capital expenses (such as new roof, tenant improvements, paving, etc.), and commission to realtors to replace tenants. What happens "below" the NOI line is what determines the ultimate yield of a real estate investment over time. For example, in the same two properties above, if the low-income tax credit housing requires $30,000 for capital improvements in a given year that leaves a net $70,000 cash flow for that year. The NNN property requires no capital improvements (or if it does, the tenant pays, so it is no expense to the owner). Therefore net income (NOI) for that year would remain $100,000, but distributable cash to the owners is much less. The less variable expenses "below" the NOI line on a profit and loss statement, the more accurately one can predict the yield and cash flow of a property over time.

Low-Income Tax Credit Housing Example

Rent Income	$200,000
Operating Expenses	$100,000
NOI	$100,000
Capital Improvements	$30,000
(tenant improvements, commissions etc.)	
Distributable Cash Flow	**$70,000**

NNN Leased Property Example

Rent Income	$100,000
Operating Expenses	$0
NOI	$100,000
Capital Improvements	$0
	(tenant pays)
Distributable Cash Flow	**$100,000**

When I received that telephone call in May 1995, I saw all investment real estate through the lens of *it was hard to create real wealth owning real estate because of all the money one had to spend to keep the income stream flowing.* That was the truth, and I had a lot of evidence to back it up. That view has since been transformed. It was valid, but not the whole truth. Later in the book, how one can transform solid views like that one will be explored. Suffice it to say, at that time it seemed real to me, so when I dove into the world of self-storage, I immediately saw something possible for myself no other type of commercial real estate offered.

Self-Storage as an Investment

I began to work with that company to find self-storage. As we located properties, I began to see how they analyze them. I helped by gathering the information from the existing owners required to forecast future cash flows (all explained in this book later). Given my paradigm, or lens through which all commercial real estate was filtered through (i.e., *it was hard to create real wealth owning real estate because of all the money one had to spend to keep the income stream flowing*), I almost immediately saw the benefits of self-storage as something to own, and my dream began.

I saw that self-storage is a steel building (sometimes block) with a concrete floor—very inexpensive to create, like most industrial buildings are. I was familiar with that type of "industrial" building. In my market at the time, industrial warehousing was generating about $3.50 per square foot gross income. I was amazed to find non-climate controlled (i.e., no heating or air conditioning) self-storage was generating $8.50 to $9.00 per square foot in the Louisville market. Climate controlled was even higher. All that rent for a steel building with a concrete floor! But I soon got the real advantage, which sent me on my adventure to figure out how a person like me could start buying self-storage: In self-storage there are **few capital improvements** required. There are **no commissions** and **no tenant improvements**. No carpet, no plumbing fixtures, and no walls to potentially re-construct every time someone moves out). There are very **predictable and schedulable capital expenditures** (paving, new roofs, etc.). The net income stream (NOI) can be projected very accurately and, with few variables pulling against it, the NOI and the distributable cash (except for the loan payments) are very close. It looked on paper very much like a NNN lease property.

I also saw that rents for self-storage can be systematically raised, and as expenses increase, the integrity of the net cash flow can be preserved. In the office buildings I was managing, the lease usually locked in rental rates for three to five years. Self-storage is a month-to-month lease. If a unit size—let's say 10' x 10'—is 90% occupied in a facility, I can raise the rents. Very few people move out, but if they do, I can usually replace them with higher-paying tenants. In fact, as I will explain later, it is part of our asset management plan to have rents rise over expense increases yearly, creating a "compounding" effect. As you will see, it is this "compounding effect" that generates the true wealth for the owners of self-storage.

In the mid-1990s I fell in love with self-storage, and I told myself: **I can do it!** Like any love affair, it has had its ups and downs, but I can with integrity say today I am more in love with it now than I was then. On December 31, 1999, I was able to close on my first facility.

However, as you will see, creating something in one's mind is only the first step. The moment a person takes a stand that something will be (like saying "I can own self-storage"), everything that is not that immediately shows up. The real challenge for a guy like me to get in the business was threefold: (1) I had to get the down payment to purchase the facilities (anywhere from $300,000 to $1.2 million per facility); (2) I had to be able to qualify for a large loan; and (3) I had to be able to purchase them so that I and anyone who gave me the down payment could get a good (above market) return on any money they gave me. Above market return is defined as a return higher than the Dow Jones or the NASDAQ stock index is generating. If you remember the 1990s the stock market was rocking and rolling.

This book chronicles how I did it, ideas for how you can do it, and shares tools you can use to fulfill this dream.

The History of Self-Storage

I was told self-storage began in Texas in the 1960s as a way for land owners with land in the path of progress to generate income from raw land as they waited for a higher and better use. However, I also found on the Internet that in 1958, Lauderdale Storage in Fort Lauderdale, Florida (founded by the Collum family) opened for business and was the first self-storage facility. I do not know which is true.

Either way, these early owners of self-storage soon realized they were achieving returns from storage that were higher than what they would get on the "higher and best use," such as shopping centers and apartments. That is when the industry begins.

Early self-storage was a pretty basic affair. Hidden in rural areas or inside industrial parks. Often camouflaged so that a passerby would not know what is there (so people's stored items would be "safe"). Often no fencing or gates, and definitely no cameras on site.

Self-storage began to grow up in the early 1970s. Public Storage was the first publicly traded company that began to "institutionalize" the industry. I remember my father talking about it when I was in high school. I think he purchased stock in the company. It sounded real dumb to me at the time (like most things adults did).

In the 1960s, self-storage unit rental rates went for around 15 cents per square foot per month. By 1985, the rate went up to 60 cents per square foot per month. In the late 1990s, rates were an average of $1 per square foot, and today rental rates can be as high as $1.50–$4 per square foot depending on the market.

As self-storage has evolved, it has become a retail type product. Locations began to move from industrial parks to retail roads. Cameras came in, and key-coded gates began to guard entrances and exits. Full premier fencing, sale of retail items (such as boxes and locks), truck rental, and managers who were trained on how to sell storage as a product became the standard.

Working for the REIT

As I began working with the REIT I learned how they conducted analysis of self-storage and what they focused on. This particular REIT was looking for first-generation facilities that could be taken to institutional grade. Ironically, one of the first facilities I looked at for this REIT was a 25,000-square-foot facility with an industrial building next door sitting on two and a half acres of land. This REIT would have purchased this facility and the property next door, but neither owner wanted to sell. I became a partner in that facility 18 years later and purchased the property next door, and we did the expansion.

> **Note:** Never throw files away. (Store them at a self-storage facility). Property *always* comes back at some time to the market.

At that time there were seven or eight large publicly traded companies. Now there are only three or four, depending on if you call U-Haul, who owns self-storage, a self-storage REIT. I also saw how these guys could create income streams where there were none and how exact they could predict income. I also saw what they could pay for self-storage. As I began to see the possibility of myself getting in this business, from the beginning I realized I would want to own something these guys would buy when I wanted to exit the property. They can move fast and pay the most.

I also had the good fortune to see how this REIT analyzed the different facilities, whether they bought them or not. When they did, I was able to see if the projects met their projections. If they did not meet their projections, I could see where and why they were off. (REITS mostly hit their targets). I actually, with their permission, began changing some formulas in their software to adjust for where I saw the mistakes were being made.

At that time, I was using (and still do) for our office management and leasing company a very sophisticated financial analysis program called Argus. In this world of self-storage, the "institutional" players were using simple Excel spreadsheets. When I went out on my own, I took the ideas I learned from the REITs, and created my own analysis program modeled more after the Argus program, but specifically for self-storage. There is a detailed chapter on how to create an analysis using this model later in the book, and the software can be viewed now at **www.CreateWealthThroughSelfStorage.com**.

After a few years of working with this REIT, it was purchased by another REIT. Before I could make a solid connection with the regional marketing director of the new REIT, the new REIT was purchased by a newer REIT. By then I had the dream, and I thought: **Now** is the time to figure out how to get in the business myself, because these guys are eating each other up, and I want to own something when there is only one or two left, and they turn their eyes away from each other.

Chapter 2
The Industry

"Change almost never fails because it's too early. It almost always fails because it's too late."
~ **Seth Godin**

The self-storage industry has grown larger than most people realize. Before we dive into how to find, analyze, and buy this product, let's get some context of the world we are getting into.

The SSA (Self Storage Association) says there are 48,500 self-storage facilities in the United States. The average size is 50,927 square feet. If we do the math, that is 2.47 billion rentable square feet. Put another way, that's 88.6 square miles of self-storage, or three times the size of Manhattan. The estimated gross revenue in 2013 was $23.9 billion. That is a lot on money.

To better show how big this industry has really become, there are only 3,510 Sears and K-Mart stores in the United States. There are a total of 4,713 Wal-Marts and Sam's Clubs in the United States. If you add up all the McDonalds, Burger Kings and Wendy's franchises in the United States, there are a total of 32,700 stores. There are 48,500 self-storage facilities. If you count all the grocery stores (with at least $2 million in annual sales), there are 32,053 in the United States.

Self-storage has become a big business, and we are still relatively new and maturing as an industry. Nine to 10% of the facilities are owned by the REITS. From my perspective, this industry may not be in its infancy, but at most we are in our teenage years.

The breakdown of ownership size is as follows:
- Owns 1 facility   63.3%
- Owns 2–4 facilities   21.2%
- Owns 5–9 facilities   5.0%
- Owns 10–24 facilities   2.5%
- Owns 25 or more facilities   9.0%

I cannot think of another industry the size of this one that is so mom and pop. More than 63% of the facilities are owned by individuals who own only one facility. Many of these are first-generation self-storage properties that at some point can be purchased and upgraded. In other words, there are still a lot of potential facilities to buy.

Here is the other area of growth for this industry. According to the SSA, 8.96% of American households currently rent a self-storage unit. That is 1 in 11 families, up from 1 in 8 families in 1990. In 1990 there were 91,900,900 families and in 2010 there were 114,800,000 (data from www.statisticbrain.com). Not to bore you with numbers, but that is a lot of new customers and this industry has barely scratched the surface with only 10% of the potential customers. There is a lot of potential growth still in this industry!

It is a good time to get in the business. I see the REITS buying more facilities from the smaller owners and re-positioning them in the

> We purchased a facility in the northern part of Houston, Texas, that was owned by a husband and wife. It was 34,000 square feet of self-storage sitting on 4.5 acres of land with a small, simple office. They never raised rents, just parked a few cars on all the extra land they owned, and never upgraded anything. They were happy with the money they made but never really looked at the full potential of the facility they had.
>
> As they aged, at some point the wife said it was time to sell. I happened to see it before the REITS did due to some relationships I had with some real estate agents in Texas. We purchased it, added another 26,000 square feet of income-producing square feet of storage units, put in truck rental, started selling tenant insurance and retail items (boxes and locks, etc.), cleaned up the existing property, and refurbished the office. I saw we could take the property from $227,000 to $508,000 by making these changes. We bought the property and are doing the expansion as I write this.

market place. An excellent exit strategy to have is to have facilities that they will look at when you are ready to exit.

What the REITS look for are facilities larger than 50,000 square feet. They want to see, or be able to create, perimeter fencing with high security features. They like truck rental and retail sales components. On average, they like 30% of the square feet to be climate-controlled space (i.e., heated and air-conditioned). They ideally like to see at least a 50,000 population within a 3-mile radius, although as they move in to second- and third-tier markets, sometimes this is not the case. REITS like to have approximately 1,200 square feet of retail and counter space at a facility. An on-site apartment for the manager is tolerated, but not created or sought out.

As we look at facilities, this is always on our minds. Can we buy or create these features with this facility so that, when the exit time comes, we will have a facility and portfolio that a REIT will at least look at? This is not the only business plan; I have seen others I like and respect. It is just our plan.

In the 1990s, one of the REITS then offered franchises. I have been a real estate franchise owner and know the value of a franchise (the systems in place, products and services already designed, and name recognition). The thinking was someone could develop a facility under their name and when they wanted to sell, the franchisor contractually has the right to step up and purchase. That concept proved not to work too well in this industry because the public saw no value in name recognition and was unwilling to pay any more to offset the franchise cost. In most industries, name recognition is a major factor in a customer deciding on a product or service. In the self-storage business, other factors are far more important.

The Customer

Ultimately, to create wealth in this business, one has to rent space to customers. A quick snapshot of the self-storage customers would be helpful in creating an acquisition strategy. This is not a book about how to appeal to the customer and run a facility so that the customers will continue leasing from you and refer other customers to you.

There are a lot of other good books and resources for that. This is a book about how to find, analyze, and purchase self-storage product to fulfill a pre-designed business strategy. The information in this chapter is designed to assist you in designing *your* business strategy.

How customers find your facility has changed over the years. When I first got in the business, more than 80% found your facility through the yellow pages. I have spent between $35,000 and $50,000 per year advertising in the yellow pages. I am here to report those days are gone!

According to the SSA, here are the national averages on how customers find a facility:

- Saw the facility by driving by   43%
- Referral   22%
- Internet/web   28%
- Line ad in yellow pages   1%
- Display ad in yellow pages   1%
- Flyer-promotional brochure   1%
- Other   2%
- Don't know   2%

After an acquisition, one should measure everything. We measure our own facilities to see where our customers come from. Here are one facility's monthly stats I just happened to review yesterday:

- Saw the facility by driving by: 20.37%
- Referral: 53.07%
- Internet/web: 22.22%
- Line add in yellow pages: 1.85%
- Display add in phone book: 0%
              (we don't have them anymore)
- Truck Rental: 1.85%
- Other   .64%
- Don't know: 0%

Each facility will vary each month or quarter, and each facility will vary from others.

Here are a few takeaways from all this information I see (I know there is more here in all this data than I see; look for it). Drive-by is usually the largest or second largest way customers find a facility. So look for a facility that has good visibility. This business has developed into a retail business, so look for retail-like locations. We have discovered that if a facility has interstate exposure, it is most likely a winner. Signage, therefore, is important as well. Retailers put a lot of resources into signage, so self-storage owners should, too.

> We offer a $25 cash referral fee to anyone who refers a customer to us who rents a unit. One of our strategies is for our managers to make friends with the other facilities in the area, and if they are full, maybe they will send someone our way. If someone does that, we always immediately run $25 cash to that person.
>
> We noticed that every Friday, we were getting at least one referral, and sometimes three to four referrals from a facility less than a mile from us. My manager told me that she was constantly running the referrals every Friday to the grandson of the owner of that facility, who ran it on Fridays. It turns out the kid needed spending money for the weekend, and referring to us gave him that money. I always wondered if the grandfather/owner ever found out what his grandson was doing.

Another takeaway for us has been referrals. For us it is usually the largest or second-largest source of business in every facility. That starts with the quality of the manager and staff (not me). Our philosophy, which may not be the best (but it is ours), is to out-pay what our competition is paying in salaries and benefits, so we can hire the best employees. Our managers receive sales and customer service training, and have targets to meet. Then we give bonuses and celebrate when their targets are hit. We offer health insurance to all full-time employees, and I am shocked that most of the rest of the industry does not. However, I believe it pays off. Look at last month's referral numbers above. Depending on the facility, I know the value of a customer (i.e., the average length of stay times the average rent). Most customers are worth $3,500 and up. Referrals are not free; they come from a good staff with good training, but in the long run they are less expensive than most other sources of business.

These statistics are provided to help you begin to design your acquisition business plan and acquisition strategy.

Another "statistic" derived from some of the above stats is that storage is rented at a rate of 1.3 units per household, and the average national unit size is approximately 120 square feet. Residential customers usually comprise 80% of a self-storage facility's customer base, and commercial customers make up 20%. With this data, you can take a look at the 3- and 5-mile radius of a facility and do a quick analysis of demand. Next, take a quick look at supply (the facility you are looking at and the competition in the three- and five-mile radius). I will do a quick analysis, but we always—100% of the time—pay an independent third party to complete a feasibility report that quantifies the supply/demand for any given submarket (more to come later). However, it is important you understand the methodology behind it. Here is one from a report I had completed in a large Southern market (the one in the northern Houston market mentioned previously).

Total Households:	2-mile:	3-mile:	5-mile:
	5,491	19,559	34,006
% of users:	9.60%	9.60%	9.60%
Total users:	527	1,878	3,265
Total units:	685	2,441	4,244
Sq. Ft. of units:	120	120	120
Residential SF (80%):	82,233	292,916	509,274
Commercial SF (20%):	20,558	73,229	127,318
Demand potential:	102,792	366,144	636,592

This facility has five competitors in the 5-mile radius, which comprise 126,900 square feet. The facility is 34,000 and we are adding an additional 26,000. So total in the market, with our proposed addition, is 187,000. What do you think? In the 3- to 5-mile radius demand is 366,144 to 636,592 square feet, and there is only an 187,000 supply? We felt very safe here going ahead with the acquisition of this facility.

Our Business Plan

In developing a sound business strategy for acquisition, holding, and disposition, these are some of the items you need to consider. There are people who know a lot more about business plan development than

I do, and they can be a resource. Use them. My intention here is to motivate you to begin thinking about and developing your strategy. In a nutshell, here are some of our major acquisition strategy points:

- Purchase a facility that is or could be expanded to meet institutional standards:
  o 50,000 square feet or more
  o Retail sales a component
  o Truck rental a component
  o Security features:
    ▪ Cameras
    ▪ Flat-screen display in retail area
    ▪ Gate code access
    ▪ Perimeter fencing
- Supply/demand has been analyzed and demand can be documented
- ___% return available to equity invested in project (8% to 12% cash on cash return, depending on factors to be discussed later)
- Own a facility a REIT would consider purchasing
- Can we turn this into the most expensive facility in the sub-market?
- Will we be proud to own this facility?

These are a few of the items on our checklist as we consider an acquisition. I know very successful people in the self-storage business who have completely different standards and checklist items.

How long are you going to own facilities? Some people buy, turn, and flip. Some own for 10-plus years. Some people will use their own money or (if you are like me) use other people's money to buy (explained later). Will you be the most expensive (i.e., best facility in a sub-market), or will you be the cheapest and offer the least rent per square foot? Both are valid approaches.

Industry Associations

The statistics in this chapter came from the Self Storage Association (SSA) unless otherwise stated.

This industry has two competing associations. Coming from the real estate industry, this seems very strange to me. I feel it is important to belong to the SSA. As much as I dislike how the political system works in our country and the way the lobby industry is able to influence decision-makers, the SSA is the organization that makes changes to benefit the self-storage industry on a state-by-state level. I would definitely join the national and state Self Storage Association.

The other association (Inside Self Storage, or ISS) has very good educational and training material, and puts on an extremely well-run national convention. They have a lot of resources self-storage owners and managers can use, such as training, support, and access to a wide variety of vendors.

Check both out for yourself and decide which one is for you. I belong to both.

Chapter 3
Creating a Problem Worthy of Your Life

"Be brave enough to start a conversation that matters."
~ Margaret Wheatley

W hat is a problem you are wrestling with right now? I do not mean being in trouble. Losing your driver's license because you have too many tickets is *trouble*. Getting fired because you are constantly coming in late is *trouble*. I mean a *problem*. What problem or *problems* do you have right now?

In my world in the mid- to late 1990s, the problem I most wrestled with professionally was generating enough steady cash flow to sustain the lifestyle that my family and I were living. As a Realtor, like most entrepreneurs, we get money only upon the successful completion of a transaction. After we have helped someone attain their goals, we get paid. I was addressing the "problem" by (1) creating property management income, where I received monthly income from managing the office buildings I was selling, and (2) increasing the size and volume of transactions brokered.

What "problems" are you dealing with right now?

Like I am now, in the 1990s and early 2000s I was continually reading, working, and taking seminars professionally and personally on attaining peak performance in my work and life. As an entrepreneur, I feel it is our responsibility to cause the next breakthrough in our ability to generate business and provide value. Our careers, our family's well-being, and the lives and families of any employees we may have are counting on it. I believe if you are creating anything of worth, especially a business, it is your responsibility to always be causing the space for the next breakthrough.

At that time, I was in a seminar and looking at what my "problem" was, as I mentioned above, and I noticed there was something very familiar with it. Over time the only thing that had changed is the number of zeros behind it (I had gone from a five- to a six-digit gross income), but I had more overhead with employees.

Is the problem you are dealing with somehow familiar? A repeat? I will bet you have had this or some version of your problem over and over.

Next, I went behind the "problem" and looked. As entrepreneurs, we do not have the luxury of having problems, solving them, and getting comfortable again. Nothing wrong with that; we just cannot afford to do that. Too much is at stake.

So I looked, and invite you to look at your "problem." What is it? Perhaps it is where the world is not meeting the expatiation or plan we have created for our professional or personal lives. In reality, there was no "problem" like a thing, like a tree, or a house. I was making money, it was going in the bank, I had customers and deals, etc. The issue was the amount of money and consistency of deposits, in my opinion, were not there. Do not get me wrong: When payroll came, and there was not enough money in the account to fund it, I was not that philosophical at that moment; I was scrambling. But the "problem" was an experience I was having internally, and it appeared to be a recurring problem, because the feeling was familiar.

Next I looked at how I dealt with the problems. I usually tried to fix them as fast as I could. Then I realized something: *Every problem I have now was the solution to another problem I had earlier.* The problem I had of getting enough money for payroll was a problem, because I hired people to do certain aspects of what I was accountable for. I had to hire them because, if I had not, there was not enough time for me to create new business as well as handle the other accountabilities I had. I was on a never-ending path. But other people are not dealing with these types of "problems," so why me? Or are they? Surely I am not that unique. So I backed it up one more step.

If we all have problems, and we are all running around fixing our problems, I thought it was time to dive into the world of "problems." I looked at them from every angle. I was sitting in a Landmark seminar one day and realized that my "belief" about problems was "problems should not be." Intellectually I understand everyone has problems, but how I act when I see a problem in my life is this: I need to solve it as fast as possible because this should not be and I need to get back to equilibrium ASAP. (If you want to see your core belief, just look at your actions around an issue).

My entire entrepreneurial experience was putting out fires: going from one problem to another, mostly dealing with lack of capital in some form or shape, solving it, taking a breath, and then running to the next area where lack of capital was showing up. On and on it went. And behind all that activity was a core belief that *problems should not exist.*

What is your core belief? Is it true?

Next I asked: Is it *true* problems should not exist? It is a valid approach from what I can see, but is it *true*?

Here is the good news! You can decide if it is true. What if I say something different? What if I said, "Everyone has problems. The quality of one's life is a function of the quality of their problems"? Just as valid.

I looked at the people I admire and then at their problems. They had big problems. Gandhi had a big problem. Martin Luther King had a big problem. I realized I was having the same boring problem over and over again.

It was time to create a new problem.

After working with the REIT, I really wanted to get into the self-storage business, but wondered how a guy with my problems could have enough money to purchase facilities. Really, let's be realistic. I may get one or two, but that would most likely be it.

I did not realize that was the belief I had until I drilled down into it, but there it was—*and I made that up.* It was valid, and it was not something to dismiss with the wave of a hand, but I realized I could replace it with something else made up that was more empowering.

I decided to create a new problem. **My new problem was I was going to be in the self-storage business in six months and I did not know how.** I knew if I failed the entire structure of my newly found empowerment was at stake.

I had helped the REIT purchase, but it is a whole new ball game when it is you.

Deal Flow

Where does one find the facilities to purchase? There is a real art to this. The best advice I can give is to work with a commercial Realtor who specializes in this product. It is a specialized product and properties that are listed with a Realtor, for the most part, are priced fairly close to their true market value. A good broker knows the current CAP rates (capitalization rates that determine the value of the cash flow; much more to come on this).

If you are determined to find the opportunities yourself, there are a few resources everyone in the self-storage business knows about. Perhaps the largest databases of commercial properties for sale are listed on a site called www.LoopNet.com. I have very strong feelings about this site, mostly negative, that are colored by my being a Realtor. I use it, but only when I have to. The data is often wrong, and anyone, including my dog, can put property on LoopNet. Often an owner wants to sell his property for let's say a million dollars, and the property is only worth five hundred thousand. Multiple Realtors have told the seller that value, so he decides to put it on LoopNet himself to "test the water."

Another source of listed property are the CIEs (commercial information exchanges) in any given market. CIEs are the listing platforms commercial Realtors use to market their property. For the most part, if a property is on a CIE, it is listed by a Realtor who knows what they are doing and the property is priced reasonably well, or the property is listed by a large developer or management company that meets guidelines the local CIE has set up. These are in essence a commercial MLS (multiple listing service) with some leeway each market uses to determine who else besides Realtors can put property on it.

There are two basic CIE companies powering the local or state CIEs in the United States: Catalyst and Excellegent. They each have a national database of all the properties in the local CIEs. One has self-storage as a separate category; the other does not. Often one must do word queries through industrial properties or through income-producing real estate to find the self-storage listings.

Then there are other sources, such as Argus (not to be confused with the institutional financial software provider). Argus is a company that supports Realtors specializing in self-storage with resources specifically designed for the industry. Again, for the most part, if a Realtor is the designated Argus representative for a market or region, you know they have the specialized knowledge necessary to market or find self-storage. My experience is they are very strong in smaller markets and less relevant in the large, tier-one markets. Many of their current listings are in smaller or rural markets now.

If you did a search today for self-storage to purchase using Google or another search engine, I am sure you would run into these sites and more. Part of your business plan should be to put in the parameters of your acquisition guidelines when you find a site that has self-storage for sale. You have developed, or are in the process of developing, those perimeters, right? Do not use mine or someone else's; it could backfire on you.

Become "The One"

Anyone getting in the business should use these resources, or develop a relationship with a Realtor who uses these sources, but these are the lowest entry level into creating deal flow. Ultimately, your success in finding good deal flow will be a function of the relationships and network you build over time. Unfortunately, there is no fast way I know of to build a successful network that generates deal flow. One has to be established as the "go-to person" for self-storage, and that takes time. Here are a few ways to begin that process. There are people who know vastly more than I do about this, so find them and use them. Here is what I know and do.

First, create a database of owners of self-storage in the market or area you want to own in. It could be state, city, MSA (Multiple Statistical Area [in other words, a city and its surrounding counties that make up the economy of that city], or regional). Lists and access to databases of specific property types, such as self-storage, are available via the Internet. At the very least, you can Google to find self-storage in a specific area. Cut and paste names and addresses of facilities. Then mail cards and letters. Every now and then, one hits an owner when they are thinking about selling. I have seen it. Mostly, however, the managers throw away those cards and letters (at least, that is my experience). However, if you are in the business to purchase, you should have a list of facilities in the markets you are interested in.

Next, join the two associations mentioned in Chapter 2 and go to their training, events, and conventions. Like all businesses, there is specialized information needed to enter and run a successful business, and you will get it there. Also, Realtors and self-storage owners are always marketing facilities at these events. The relationships you establish will be ones you use throughout your career in the business. I have established long-lasting relationships with self-storage manufacturers, website providers, Realtors, marketing companies, and more after meeting them at conventions. I lean on these relationships daily.

Even if you are not a social media person, join or create groups on LinkedIn that deal with self-storage. I think, although I am in no way a specialist on this topic, a valid approach is to post content (or re-post articles you can find) that shows you are in the business. It at least gives the appearance you know what you are doing. I think the goal would be to show up as a specialist and develop online relationships, so that when someone has a specific need, you are a go-to person for them.

Over the years, it has gotten to the point that almost every day my e-mail in box has some new storage listing or land that could be a self-storage facility. I have different websites set up to automatically send me information on new listings, and I have opted in to many companies and people who market storage or related services.

Unfortunately, so does everyone else who is serious about acquiring storage facilities. In reality, we are all competing for the same inventory at any given moment. The person or group that can respond the quickest and give the seller the best perceived value wins. Sometimes through your network you will find a property before it hits the market, but it will be hard to stake a career on the number of off market facilities one runs across. Ultimately your success will be how fast and accurately you can analyze a self-storage facility listed for sale and how successful you are at negotiating.

It takes time, but get in front of as much deal flow as you can. The rest of this book and the resources available through it will support you and give you the ability to react fast, but without a property to analyze or compete for, nothing happens.

Final Thoughts

At this stage of my career, competing against the REITS now in the larger markets is my greatest challenge. These guys are hungry to buy, can pay a lot, and close quickly. However, my business plan includes owning facilities in larger markets, so I have developed strategies I will explain to successfully compete with REITs. It all begins with finding the deals first, however.

After you buy your first facility or two, Realtors will begin to seek you out. If you become known as a buyer—someone who makes decisions and can execute—as opposed to a looker, you will get in front of deals.

So create a new problem for yourself. Have a facility you want to buy, but are not sure what to do next. That is a worthy problem to have. That is probably a lot more interesting and exciting than your usual problems.

Chapter 4
APPLICATION: A New Problem

"You miss 100% of the shots you don't take."
~ Wayne Gretzky

In 2012, I had a problem. I was back in the self-storage business and created a goal of putting together a $60,000,000 self-storage portfolio I would have ownership in, manage, and be able to control to a large degree. I had started in 1999 and quickly started putting together a portfolio. I had put two properties together quickly and was working on my third. Then I received an unsolicited offer from a regional REIT for the portfolio. I did not want to sell, but our partnership documents at the time said it took a simple majority vote to sell the properties. The offer was so good, the partners at the time said, "Let's take it!"

I was out of the business as quickly as I got in. I was not going to make that mistake again. Back then I had a good deal with about 20 percent of ownership and the management of the facilities with fees that generated. My mistake was I did not anticipate how quickly the value would rise as we raised rents and as the market heated up. So this time, my approach getting in the business was very different.

I was not a person with a lot of money or from a wealthy family, so if I was going to be in the self-storage business, I had to use other people's money and yet have enough control so the same thing wouldn't happen again. It took me until 2007 before I could get back in. The first property I purchased getting back in is the case study later in the book.

However, by 2012, I had two properties in the portfolio, close to

$9,000,000 of value at the time. We were emerging from a recession that had hit many of us hard. Self-storage fared pretty well, only losing about 6% of occupancy, but the rest of the commercial real estate industry—where I received most of my income—did not fare as well. I had gone 18 months with no real estate commission income, living off the small income I was making in self-storage at the time and my savings.

I had a problem. I had a goal ($60,000,000 self-storage portfolio) and was not progressing very fast toward it. When I did find a property I liked, REITS or larger players would usually outbid me. They could pay more than I could because their cost of funds is lower. In order for me to raise the equity, I had to offer the investors 10% to 12% return on their investment and to purchase facilities that would generate that return. I was easily outbid.

In the world of problems, this was a better problem to have than many I could have had.

The Next Self-Storage Facility

In 2009 I saw on LoopNet a facility for sale that I was very familiar within our market. It was one that had expressway exposure and was very visible. I had admired it for many years every time I drove by. I was surprised to see it listed for sale. It was not listed with a broker and the owner had put it on LoopNet to "see what would happen" (one of the many problems with LoopNet, in my opinion). Later I learned this property was owned by two people: a "money" person and a "manager," who constructed it and ran it. They had also done the same with a self-storage facility in Florida. In 2009 the Florida property was apparently not doing well, and the two owners made the decision to test the market with the facilities.

One of the unusual things about this was it was on a land lease. That means the two owners of the self-storage facility do not own the land the facility sits on; someone else does. They lease the land from the land owner, and build their buildings on the leased land. Having been in real estate, I knew land leases scared a lot of people and many people would not even consider a property with one. Under certain circumstances, a land lease would not bother me because ultimately one is merely buying cash flows anyway. If I dug into the deal and did not like the land lease aspect, I could always walk. So in 2009 I made a run at the property by writing a letter of intent to purchase based on the income and expense numbers the "managing" partner provided. (I was unaware of the "money" partner at that time). I thought I must have offended the guy because he never responded to my letter and did not answer my calls. I quickly forgot about it, because writing offers that get "no thank you" or no response at all is very common.

By 2012 I had developed another self-storage facility in that market (thus I owned two facilities), expanding my sphere of influence, and I was becoming known as the guy who knew about self-storage in the commercial real estate network there. I ended up meeting and knowing someone who knew the "money" partner in the facility from 2009. He told me that this person was extremely savvy and was invested in many businesses and enterprises. This self-storage facility was just a minor investment he was in. He had made his money being the first franchisee of a very successful restaurant chain. I was told in that conversation in the summer of 2012 that the "money" guy, who was in his 60s, had his entire restaurant chain under contract for some high number, approaching $100 million.

This is not uncommon for people who have made great wealth to begin to start disposing of assets in their 60s as they begin to wind down. I thought if he would sell his restaurants perhaps he would sell his self-storage. I did not want to make the mistake of going through the "managing" partner this time. I guessed, and it was later confirmed, that the "money" partner would most likely make the decisions, anyway, even if they were 50/50 owners. So I asked the friend who knew the "money" partner to set up a lunch with me. My friend and both partners showed up to the lunch.

It really works to build up your network of people you know. This might occur like a random event, but it is really years of work and working in the industry that gave me the creditability so that the "money" partner would meet with me. Build your network. You never know who knows whom.

It turned out that the "money" partner was interested in disposing of his assets, but indicated no "deal" was going to happen. If he was going to sell, he wanted to sell on an 8% CAP rate, and whoever purchased had to assume the loan they had on the property. When I asked why, he indicated he had a conduit loan (more about loans later in book). That is a non-recourse loan (a loan that owners do not have to personally guarantee). For the purposes here, let's say the loan had a large pre-payment penalty. He did not want to pay the penalty, and he wanted a "good" price.

What would you think? Probably what I thought: How much was this lunch going to cost me? However, I did not have all the current income and expense numbers, and I knew if they did not sell then, at some time they would be sellers. I know all property comes around for sale at some time, so I in no way wanted to alienate them. I indicated I was excited to be exploring the property and was honored that they would share their numbers with me. I assured them if it was anywhere close to what I could pay, I would jump on the opportunity and I could perform. I had no idea how or who would be the investors, or how in the world I could ever "qualify" for a Wall Street loan assumption, but that was not my problem at that moment. In fact, that would be a better problem to have than the one I had, which was no deal flow.

I bought lunch.

As I left, I saw what appeared to be a heated discussion between the partners outside as I walked by. It appeared to me the "manager" in no way wanted to sell. He had a good thing going. The "money" guy was saying something to the effect of "If we can get a good price now, we are going to sell". I usually don't want to be the guy who pays that "good price"; I have overpaid for things in the past and it is not that much fun.

So I got in the car, licked my wounds. and went back to work. I doubted anything was going to come of the meeting, but I was interested to see their numbers. I wondered how they may have changed since 2009.

What they sent me was very surprising. I had heard the figure $6.5 million for a value of the facility thrown around at the lunch by the "money" partner. My internal dialogue when I heard that was "good luck." But when I saw their 2011 net income (total income less operating expenses) from their profit and loss statement, it was $248,100 net income. However, included in the expenses was $194,116 for the land lease expense and $133,640 of interest. Back those out of expenses, and there was a NOI (net operating income) of $575,587. 2012 was on track to be even better. Take the $575,587 and divide it by .08 (the 8% CAP the "money" partner indicated was a line in the sand), and you get a value more than $7 million. They were paying more than $50,000 a year in Yellow Pages and a few other expenses that appeared like ones I may not have or be able to reduce.

All of the sudden the cost of that lunch did not bother me quite as much.

One never knows what will turn up. The loan balance was just slightly more than $2 million, so I had to raise a lot of equity and had no idea if I could, or how it would look financially to an investor, but I had a potential deal to work with. This was more than I had the day before. So I quickly wrote a letter of intent (LOI) for the $6.5 million they wanted, indicating I would assume the loan. My goal was to get this property standing still and under my control. It still was a long shot, but at least I had a potential project to work on.

Given the complexity of this deal with the Wall Street loan, the defeasance (Defeasance is the cost of putting another institutional-grade investment instrument in lieu of the loan, generating the same return as the paid-off loan did for the buyer of the loan package sold on Wall Street.), and the land lease, I searched for a lawyer who could assist me in writing the contract after the sellers accepted the LOI, and I began working on the financial analysis.

I had a new problem: I only had 60 days to do everything and close on the property.

Chapter 5
A First Look at How to Analyze Self-Storage

*"I am not a product of my circumstances.
I am a product of my decisions."*
~ Stephen Covey

So now you have a facility you want to look at purchasing. What next? Here is the fun part. You must figure out what you will pay for it, and most likely compete with many other people doing the same thing. Now we are getting into what I feel will give you the best competitive edge in the business. The financial analysis software, The Valuator, available through the website associated with this book (www.CreatingWealthThroughSelfStorage.Com), is one of, if not the best available in this business. This analysis software has evolved over the years and allows me to quickly see the cash flows, cash on cash return for the investors, and breakeven point of occupancy, as well as quantify the risk. Based on what return someone wants, or the cost of equity (the return needed for the investors), one can determine quickly what can be paid for a facility.

Here is a tip: People in most cases will talk about the size of a self-storage facility in number of units. "This facility has 480 units." Interesting, but irrelevant. Begin to think in terms of square feet when relating to size. Most management software for facilities has both now, but square feet is the accurate way to think and complete your analysis. I am not that interested in how many units I am renting; I am very interested in the square feet I have rented. A 5' x 5' unit and a 20' x 40' unit are both units, but vastly different in area-generating income.

How to Analyze a Self-Storage Facility

If the property is listed, usually the listing agent has a marketing package. Most marketing packages have an executive summary in narrative form that discusses the history of the facility and something about its position in the marketplace. As I read it, I look for (1) why is owner selling, (2) does the facility have a problem, and (3) if it does, do I have the skill set to solve the problem? I am also looking for the physical occupancy and the economic occupancy. Simply put, "physical occupancy" is how much of the facility is occupied, and "economic occupancy" is how much of the facility is paying rent. Let's say 88% of the square feet of a facility are rented, but only 72% or so are generating income. That is a problem you can fix in most cases. If that information is not in the marketing package, it is one of the questions I will ask. I suggest you create a list of questions and call once (no more than twice) to the agent or owner; that shows you know what you are doing.

I am looking in the narrative for the motivation of the Seller to sell and if there are any problems. If I cannot figure it out, I ask. Is there a lot of deferred maintenance? If so, I will calculate a number I need to invest. Is it below the market in rent? Is it below the market in occupancy? Is it higher in rent or occupancy than the other self-storage facilities in the market? If there is no information in the marketing package about other facilities nearby, I actually drive to the competition and try to get a handle on it. You do not have to figure everything out exactly, because the feasibility report you are going to order (discussed later) will tell you exactly about your competition and your position in the market

Note: When renting units, doors are very important. The door is the only moving part, and my suggestion is to have the doors open quietly and smoothly. We do whatever it takes to have the doors work correctly and not get jammed up, even if I have to replace them. When a manager shows a space in a facility we own, it is (very) clean (walls washed, back of roll-up door clean, floor mopped or painted if stained) and the doors open quietly and smooth. After every move-out, the manager or maintenance teams do door maintenance with lithium spray, check tracks and rollers, as well as spring tension.

where the facility is located. You do want to get a *feel* for the facility you are considering purchasing in relation to the nearby competition. Sometimes I rent a unit in the facility I am considering or in a competing facility to go through the rental process, and see the staff and the contract. I then am late in paying to see how the late notices go out and how effective they are in collecting.

I very much like finding facilities where there is a greater than 8% gap between physical and economic occupancy (we are able to keep that between 3% and 5% with how we manage). That is a problem I can fix fairly fast with a good property management team and systems in place. I also look for the condition of the doors and units. If you find a facility where there is a gap between physical and economic occupancy, you are probably going to find there has not been a lot of ongoing door maintenance and cleaning. If the owner is not taking care of the business, they are probably not taking care of the facility.

Finally in the narrative, I am looking for any hint of the seller's motivation for selling. This will help me in the negotiation. If you look at the numbers from Chapter 2, you will see a lot of facilities are owned by people who just have one facility. As these people age and/ or change their life circumstance, a certain percentage of them will go on the market. I love buying those, because in many cases those owners got comfortable with whatever cash flow they were receiving and may have not kept up with the industry trends. Often these owners have left a lot of potential income streams untapped, which just needs proper management and/or repositioning of the facility in the current market climate to reap. That is why REITS can pay so much for a facility. They have figuring out how much money they can generate from a facility down to a science, and they can pay a high price and still make good money. *(See the insert story on page 18 again.)*

Then from there, I jump into the financial analysis.

Financial Analysis Starting Point

Unit Mix Page

The analysis always starts with the unit mix and current pricing. I immediately look in the package for that sheet. I want to see how many 5' x 5' units the facility has, how many 10' x 10's, and so forth, and the current street rate for each size. Many marketing packages or sellers do not think to provide that information for some reason. If it is not there, nothing happens until I get it. All of the analysis starts there. I fill that form out, and then I stop and look. Much of what I need to know comes from this page. Below is a unit mix page from the facility in the Houston area we purchased. As I looked at it after I spent the 10 minutes filling in the unit size, how many of each, and the asking price of each, I could see where the upside was.

Exhibit Number 1: Unit Mix - Existing

	Unit Size	Unit S.F.	#Units	Total S.F.	% of Total S.F.	Monthly Unit Price	Annual Rent/S.F.	Monthly GPI	Annual GPI
Existing Units NCC	5 x 10	50	28	1,400	4.09%	$50.00	$12.00	$1,400	$16,800
	10 x 10	100	26	2,600	7.60%	$70.00	$8.40	$1,820	$21,840
	10 x 15	150	24	3,600	10.53%	$80.00	$6.40	$1,920	$23,040
	10 x 20	200	16	3,200	9.36%	$100.00	$6.00	$1,600	$19,200
	10 x 25	250	12	3,000	8.77%	$130.00	$6.24	$1,560	$18,720
	10 x 30	300	10	3,000	8.77%	$145.00	$5.80	$1,450	$17,400
Total NCC Storage			116	16,800	49.12%		$6.96	$9,750	$117,000
Existing Units CC	5 x 10	50	24	1,200	3.51%	$69.00	$16.56	$1,656	$19,872
	10 x 10	100	36	3,600	10.53%	$100.00	$12.00	$3,600	$43,200
	10 x 15	150	48	7,200	21.05%	$115.00	$9.20	$5,520	$66,240
	10 x 20	200	18	3,600	10.53%	$160.00	$9.60	$2,880	$34,560
	10 x 30	300	6	1,800	5.26%	$260.00	$10.40	$1,560	$18,720
Total CC Storage			132	17,400	50.88%		$10.49	$15,216	$182,592
Outside Parking	Parking		20			$45.00		$900.00	$10,800.00
Total Parking			20					$900.00	$10,800.00
Total Income:			248	34,200	100.00%		$8.76	$25,866	$310,392.00

Average S.F. @ Unit	137.9
Net Rentable S.F.	34,200

I first look at what percentage is climate controlled and non–climate controlled. This facility is 50.88% climate controlled (very high). As I looked at the other facilities in the sub-market where this facility was located, I saw that no one else had any climate controlled units. This facility was more than 90% occupied (physically), so the market liked this high percentage. I liked it too, because it was generating $10.40 per square foot

Note: In my experience I have found four reasons why there is a large discrepancy in the physical and economic occupancy: (1) a large variance in the rates a unit of the same size is being charged (i.e., a 10′ x 10′ unit has 20 different rates being paid). This usually occurs when, as price increases are implemented, the current customer keeps his or her current rate; (2) rates are reduced as incentives to move in; (3) poor collection practices (i.e., people are occupying a unit but no income is coming in); and (4) the manager or owner is taking money. (Sometimes owners or managers pocket cash, for example, and do not report it.) My experience is in most cases it is a combination of numbers 1 and 2. You can set up safeguards for most of the ways number 4 can happen.

as opposed to non–climate controlled space generating $6.96 per square foot. (The industry average is 30% or so climate-controlled space for institutional grade self-storage).

I really like this opportunity because, as you can see, the existing facility had 34,200 square feet of existing self-storage, and there is enough expansion land to generate an additional 26,000 square feet of new space, getting me more than the 50,000 square foot threshold that is part of our business plan. I very much like opportunities where I get existing cash flow while I generate new ones.

I also saw the rents were not particularly high and it appears as if I can raise them. As I looked at the rents of my competition, this bore out, although not a steep hike is possible. Then I saw the gross potential income of $310,392 (is if every unit was rented and every unit paid) of the existing units there.

You will get to the point where this form will tell you about the health of the facility and the upside. I quickly glanced at the marketing package and looked at the income they showed for the facility in the previous year, and then divided that number by the gross potential income. I could see that the economic occupancy was 78.32% and the physical was 88%.

In "The Self-Storage Valuator" software, on the unit mix page, just fill out the unit size, number of units of each, and the current asking price. The program fills out the rest and populates the other relevant pages with the relevant data from this page. *Everything starts here. Take whatever steps you need to have this page filled out correctly.*

Assumptions Page

The next page to fill out is the assumptions page. Although this page is quick, it is also very important. Do not rush through this page. Here are some of my assumptions, and ones I used on this facility. I knew the asking price, so I determined the purchase price as a number very close to it (95%). This was a hot market, and lots of others were looking. I usually start with their asking price, but here I knew I could discount it somewhat. Next I assumed I could raise rents at least 3% per year (income increase). I also assumed expenses would go up 2.5% (expense increase). Then I filled out the loan information. I was going to raise 35% equity (down payment), so the loan to value (LTV) was 65%. I knew at the time the interest rate was close to 4.65% and I could get a 20-year amortization. Most banks will have call, or balloon payment, due in three, five, or seven years. I used five. (Other than SBA loans, there are very few if any self-amortizing commercial loans out there.) There are a few other assumptions to fill out (details later in the book and on **www.CreatingWealthThrough SelfStorage.com**. I also put in $35,000 for initial maintenance expense to clean up and refresh the existing facility. "Disposition CAP rate" is perhaps the most subjective number in this section of the program. You are guessing what the future capitalization rates will be. I usually make it higher than my acquisition CAP rate. So if I am purchasing on an 8% CAP, I will use 8.5% or 9.0% as a disposition. (See Chapter 2, or use **www.CreatingWealthThroughSelf Storage.com** for further information on CAP rates).

For stabilized occupancy I use as 85%. Stabilized occupancy is the average occupancy per year a facility will achieve once it has gone through the lease up period and is a mature project where the move ins and the move outs are roughly equal each month. There may be seasonal differences, but on a yearly average, what that occupancy number is for a facility is, that is stabilized occupancy. For facilities over 50,000 square feet, the industry average has been around 85%. I use that 85% stabilized occupancy number for two reasons: (1) Throughout the history of self-storage, 85% has been the historic stabilized rate (although that is changing upward at the time of this writing), and (2) banks still use it in their underwriting. If the project works at 85%, it will work at 90%. Ultimately your feasibility report will tell you what stabilized occupancy to use.

> *Note:* I am going to say this over and over in this book. Here is the real secret for creating wealth in self-storage. It is also the real art of "asset management". We strive to have our income increase 1% to 2% per year over operating expenses. You will see on the 10-year cash flow page, the *compounding effect* this practice has. (In my Financial Analysis I just use .5%, or half a percent). If you raise a $100-per-month unit 3%, it goes to $103. Few customers will move out of a unit for a $3 difference, and if they do, gladly let them so you can replace them with higher-paying customers. I am amazed at the number of owners who resist raising rents out of fear of losing customers. This is where the real wealth is created.

Here is a summary of the fields to populate on this page for a standard self-storage facility acquisition:
- Purchase price
- Closing cost
  - Legal fees
  - Feasibility report
  - Closing cost
- Annual revenue growth
- Annual expense growth
- Initial capital improvements
- Permanent financing
  - Loan to value (LTV)

- o   Interest rate
- o   Annual interest
- o   Amortization
- o   Note call date
- The program will take this information and generate all the pages. The only other assumptions that may be required are construction estimates if it is new construction or if you are contemplating an expansion. This will be covered in a later chapter.

Operating Expenses

The last page to fill out in a standard acquisition (i.e., you are not building or expanding a facility, just purchasing what is there and its cash flow) is the operating expenses page. Many of the expenses I can get directly from the seller or the marketing package. On the ten year cash flow page, all expenses are categorized into eight categories. The operating expenses page is where they are detailed. They translate over to the 10-year cash flow page inside their categories.

1. **Advertising:** I look at what they are spending on advertising. The most important question is: Do they have yellow pages? If I cannot tell, I ask. If they do, how long is their contract? I am going to eliminate it, or at the least cut it back drastically. (Less and less facilities are using it anymore). I know my cost for a website (find out yours), and I will usually budget some key ad word and pay-per-click money, and some other funds for referrals and events.

2. **Personnel:** I look at what they are spending, but I have my own philosophy on employees. Your business plan will inform you whether you want to pay at the top range of the spectrum for storage employees or toward the lower end. Are you going to be the manager? If the facility is more than 50,000 square feet, we usually have a full-time manager who gets benefits (we pay health insurance and 401(K) retirement benefits), a part-time manager to

cover on days off, sick days, and usually one day overlap so the manager can market or work in the facility. We own more than one facility, so this "part-time" manager is really full time—just part time for that facility. They will rotate from facility to facility to cover days off. We also schedule a fixed number of hours per week for a maintenance person to work. You, however, may have the manager do the maintenance work. Fill out this section based on your strategy for a facility.

3. **Repairs and Maintenance:** I usually look at what they have been spending. I also know in my facilities what I have been spending. If you do not have a track record to use, look at what they are reporting and compare it to the industry standard. Use the higher number between the two.

4. **Insurance:** I usually use their number and raise it a little.

5. **Utilities:** I usually use their number and raise it a little.

6. **Property Taxes:** Be careful here. They will usually report what they are paying in property taxes. You need to put what you will be paying, which is usually based on the acquisition price. I have made the mistake more than once of underestimating property tax. I usually have to research and find, or ask the selling agent, how that tax rate is assessed in that locality of the facility, which is determined by the taxing authority.

7. **Other:** Here is all the stuff you will pay that is rarely reported in a marketing package (stamps, office supplies, credit card expense, dumpsters, etc.). If you don't know, guess to the best of your ability or use industry averages if reported.

8. **Management Fee:** Part of our strategy is to charge for management. You may hire a third-party management company, or you may self-manage and not charge. My experience is that lenders underwrite using a management fee (because they would have to pay it if they foreclose), so

even if you are going to manage yourself, I suggest putting something here. I have also seen owners distribute cash to themselves under this line item because they can write it off as an expense for the facility.

As you grow in this business, you will have some per-square-foot averages you can rely on to use for certain operating expense figures. When I was starting out and did not have any other facilities to use as a reference, I used the data published yearly by the associations. *Self Storage Almanac* is a very good reference. I still receive *Self Storage Almanac* to compare my averages with the rest of the industry. The operating expenses page takes perhaps the longest for me to fill out because it forces me to think through my strategy for a particular facility. However, the good news is I am done after I fill out this page (unless I am doing an expansion or building from ground up, in which case there are two more pages to fill out).

Ten-Year Cash Flow Page

Now, after all this work, look at the 10-year cash flow page. This will tell the complete story. I study the entire page, but when I look at it for the first time, my eyes go directly to the Net Operating Income line in year one. It is usually lower (much) than the seller has projected. However, that is not a problem for me. I base my decisions to purchase not off a CAP rate of this number alone. I am interested in how much cash is being generated after debt service and reserves, and what the return on the equity invested (ROI) is. That informs me how well this project will work for our business plan. Although making acquisition decisions based on my "going in" CAP rate is valid, I rarely if ever use it as my decision to purchase. I have other criteria (discussed later in book).

Your business plan and this page will inform you if this deal will work. If it doesn't, adjust the acquisition price until it does. That will tell you what you can pay for the facility to achieve your desired return.

Over the years, I have evolved this analysis software. I can authentically say it is the best analysis tool in the industry. It has saved my tail numerous times and I can say with integrity that I have exceeded the 10-year cash flow statement every time in my career except once. In fact, as you will see, I am so confident about the information on this page, I will attach it to my LLC documents and guarantee I will hit within 85% to 90% of the numbers on this page, in any given year, or my partners can replace me as the manager of the facility (**I am not suggesting you do that**. I do it based on my confidence in the numbers *I* generated on this page).

> *Note:* As a Realtor, I have had clients where I filled out this financial analysis for them. Big mistake. If you are a commercial real estate agent using this program, let the client fill out the assumptions and as many of the pages as possible. This program can create an accurate reflection of the future of the project if you execute the plan associated with this financial program. I had a client where I assumed they would spend $80,000 to upgrade the facility, thus being able to generate higher income. They did not spend the $80,000 but expected the higher income.

We will continue to update this program as the industry evolves and as we see places where it can be improved. If you are a purchaser, you will get the updates at no additional cost or expense; they will automatically be there for you. Also, if there is something you see that would improve the tool for you, do not hesitate to reach out to us via the web site.

We will look in greater detail at how to interpret what is generated on the various pages, but this chapter was the starting point when one comes across a facility. The majority of times I end up stopping here because most facilities are priced higher than I can afford to pay and don't meet my business plan. I will always get to the price I think I can pay, and if it is drastically lower, rather than waste my time writing an offer, I will have a conversation with the agent or owner and share my thoughts. If you listen, it is not hard to see if your value has a chance of being a price the seller will accept.

Using this form, I can, in less than an hour, determine if this is a self-storage I want to pursue. If so, I begin to execute the basic steps of purchasing a self-storage facility:

1. Find a self-storage facility for sale or possibly for sale.
2. Do preliminary analysis (outlined in this chapter).
3. Decide if I can afford the facility.
4. Write an offer:
    a. Usually start with LOI (letter of intent) where basic business terms of offer are negotiated.
    b. Move to after accepted LOI or, if market is hot and I am close to seller's value in my analysis, start with a contract.
   (If contract is accepted.)
5. Start the due diligence period:
    a. Order feasibility report.
    b. Order physical inspections.
    c. Do my financial due diligence.
    d. Update the Valuator financial analysis with actual numbers replacing my assumptions as I complete inspections.
    e. Apply for loan.
6. If everything works out through due diligence period, close and take ownership of the facility.

We will go through these together in this book. For me it always begins and ends with this analysis tool. I update it as I get access to actual numbers during the due diligence period. Then I and my partners look at the final updated analysis and decide if we are going to purchase. If we decide yes, to this date, I have been fortunate enough to get every facility we have had under contract. We are usually the ones who will walk over items discovered during inspections, or over items revealed in the feasibility report.

Let's assume you have found a property, completed a preliminary analysis, and think you have a value you can pay that the seller will accept. We will move on from there now.

Chapter 6
APPLICATION: What to Do?

"I have no special talents. I am only passionately curious."
~ Albert Einstein

After I had the accepted LOI on the property discussed in Chapter 4 from the two partners, I forwarded all the relevant information to an attorney who I felt could draft a contract. I also went to work on an analysis so I could go out and raise the money.

As stated in Chapter 5, I started with the unit mix page.

Exhibit Number 2: Unit Mix - Existing

	Unit Size	Unit S.F.	# Units	Total S.F.	% of Total S.F.	Monthly Unit Price	Annual Rent/S.F.	Monthly GPI	Annual GPI
	5 x 5	25	20	500	0.50%	$45.00	$21.60	$900	$10,800
	5 x 10	50	73	3,650	3.64%	$70.00	$16.80	$5,110	$61,320
	5 x 10	50	2	100	0.10%	$80.00	$19.20	$160	$1,920
	10 x 10	100	126	12,600	12.58%	$109.00	$13.08	$13,734	$164,808
	10 x 15	150	74	11,100	11.08%	$134.00	$10.72	$9,916	$118,992
Existing Units NCC	10 x 20	200	118	23,600	23.56%	$159.00	$9.54	$18,762	$225,144
	12 x 20	240	5	1,200	1.20%	$189.00	$9.45	$945	$11,340
	10 x 25	250	57	14,250	14.23%	$179.00	$8.59	$10,203	$122,436
	14 x 20	280	1	280	0.28%	$199.00	$8.53	$199	$2,388
	10 x 30	300	45	13,500	13.48%	$199.00	$7.96	$8,955	$107,460
	12 x 25	300	6	1,800	1.80%	$199.00	$7.96	$1,194	$14,328
	12 x 30	360	5	1,800	1.80%	$219.00	$7.30	$1,095	$13,140
	10 x 40	400	1	400	0.40%	$299.00	$8.97	$299	$3,588
	14 x 30	420	1	420	0.42%	$299.00	$8.54	$299	$3,588
Total NCC Storage			534	85,200	85.05%		$10.11	$71,771	$861,252

	Unit Size	Unit S.F.	# Units	Total S.F.	% of Total S.F.	Monthly Unit Price	Annual Rent/S.F.	Monthly GPI	Annual GPI
Existing Units CC	5 x 5	25	27	675	0.67%	$49.00	$23.52	$1,323	$15,876
	5 x 10	50	44	2,200	2.20%	$85.00	$20.40	$3,740	$44,880
	10 x 10	100	41	4,100	4.09%	$158.00	$18.96	$6,478	$77,736
	10 x 15	150	10	1,500	1.50%	$175.00	$14.00	$1,750	$21,000
	10 x 20	200	31	6,200	6.19%	$225.00	$13.50	$6,975	$83,700
	15 x 20	300	1	300	0.30%	$250.00	$10.00	$250	$3,000
Total CC Storage			154	14,975	14.95%		$16.44	$20,516	$246,192
Outside Parking	10 x 20		90			$49.00		$4,410.00	$52,920.00
	10 x 25		59			$59.00		$3,481.00	$41,772.00
	10 x 35		23			$85.00		$1,955.00	$23,460.00
	10 x 40		27			$99.00		$2,673.00	$32,076.00
	20 x 30		1			$155.00		$155.00	$1,860.00
	10 x 30		27			$69.00		$1,863.00	$22,356.00
Total Parking			227					$14,537.00	$174,444.00
Total In-come:			688	100,175	100.00%		$11.06	$86,308	$1,281,888.00

Average S.F. @ Unit	145.6
Net Rentable S.F.	100,175

This site was sitting on 11 acres of leased land. The first thing I noticed was the number of parking spaces and how much income it generated. There were 227 parking spaces with a potential of over $14,500 monthly. On the 11 acres were 100,175 square feet of net rentable units and, combined with the parking, $86,308 gross potential income per month. Their occupancy was in excess of 90% and their economic occupancy was about 4% behind the physical. This was a well-run facility.

I next noticed there were only 14,975 square feet of climate-controlled units, or 14.95% of the square footage. We usually like to have around 30%, so if we ever expanded, we could build the type of space that generates more money per square foot. In this case, they were getting $16.44 psf gross potential income on the climate-controlled space (the highest I had seen to date).

Next I entered the assumptions.

Exhibit Number 3: Project Cost

PROJECT COST					
Acquisition Cost					
Facility Cost	100,000	$65.00	100,175	$64.89	$6,500,000
Closing Cost					$5,000
Legal Fees		$0.25		$0.25	$25,000
Environmental Study		$0.02		$0.02	$2,000
Assumption/Lending Fees		$0.28		$0.28	$28,000
Total Acq. Cost	100,000	$65.60	100,175	$65.49	$6,560,000
TOTAL PROJECT COST	100,000	$65.60	100,175	$65.49	$6,560,000

Annual Rev. Growth	2.50%
Annual Expense Growth	2.00%
Initial Capital Improvements	$250,000
Acquisition Cap Rate	8.75%
Stabilized Econ. Occ.	85%
Reversion Cap Rate	9.00%
Permanent Financing	
Debt	$3,000,000
LTV Ratio	80%
Rate	5.25%
Amortization	20

I hated the fact I was going to have to assume this loan. It was 5.25% and only had about a $2 million loan balance. It was also expensive with a loan assumption fee and all the legal cost involved. I thought I would deal with the loan aspect of this deal last; if the rest of project worked, I would figure something out.

Inflation had been under 2.5% for the last couple of years, so I used that figure in the expense growth, and felt I was very safe with a 3% income growth per year average. CAP rates at the time were well below 9%, but given this was on a land lease, and I did not know what CAP rates may be in future, I safely used 9% as the CAP rate to determine future values ("disposition CAP rate").

Next I put in my expenses, based on the 2011 P & L, I had received from the seller and a little adjusting on my part.

Exhibit Number 4: Projected Operating Expenses

PROJECTED OPERATING EXPENSES YEAR 1						
					Annual @ Year 1	
ADVERTISING						
Yellow Pages					$7,200	
Web					$3,540	
Other					$3,000	
TOTAL					**$10,740**	
PERSONNEL						
	Employee	Hr./Wk.	Rate/Hr.	Total/Wk.		
	Primary	40	$15.00	$600.00		
	Assistant	40	$12.00	$480.00		
	Supervisor	15	$10.00	$150.00		
	Maint.	0	$0.00	$0.00		
				$1,230.00		
Salaries					$65,190	
Bonus/Ryder					$2,000	
Payroll Taxes				14.00%	$9,127	
Insurance W/C					$ -	
Health Insurance					$5,000	
TOTAL					**$81,317**	
REPAIRS & MAINTENANCE						
Building					$6,000	
Equipment					$1,200	
Grounds					$5,300	
Parking Lot					$4,000	
Snow Removal					$4,100	
Security					$3,000	
TOTAL					$23,600	

PROJECTED OPERATING EXPENSES YEAR 1		
INSURANCE		
Liability	$3,000	
Property	$8,000	
TOTAL	$11,000	
TRUCK		
Insurance	$2,000	
Gas	$500	
Repairs	$1,500	
TOTAL	**$4,000**	
UTILITIES		
Electric/Gas	$13,000	
Water/Sewer	$1,000	
TOTAL	$14,000	
LOCAL & PROPERTY TAX	**$50,000**	
OTHER		
Bank Service/VISA Chg.	$20,000	
Computer Support/Supplies	$5,000	
Dues and Subscriptions	$1,000	
Legal & Accounting	$2,500	
Foreclosure	$3,500	
Inventory	$2,100	
Postage	$1,000	
Printing/Copies	$1,500	
Supplies	$3,800	
Telephone	$4,000	
Trash	$4,200	
TOTAL	**$48,600**	
MANAGEMENT FEE 4.50%	**$49,257**	
TOTAL PROJECTED OPERATING EXPENSES - YEAR 1	**$292,514**	**$2.92**
MONTHLY:	**$24,376**	

I made a mistake here. It was not until later, after contract and in the due diligence period, that I realized the "managing" partner had executed a one-year contract with the yellow pages for more than $25,000 per year for the next 12 months. I had to assume that contract.

I also used a higher personnel figure than he paid and a lower management fee than we usually charge, but one I felt was needed because I could get a third-party management firm in at that rate for a property this size (4.5% of gross income instead of the usual 6% of gross income).

After inputting all of that data, I immediately saw that (1) I wanted the facility, and (2) I did not want to assume that loan. After putting in a cost for the land lease of $194,116 per year, I was showing in year one a net operating income (NOI) of $611,975, or at a 9% CAP a property with a value of $6.8 million I was purchasing for $6.5 million fully stabilized. I just had one problem: I had to raise so much cash (difference between loan assumption and sales price), my cash on cash return was below 8% in the first few years, and I knew no one I knew was going to get too excited about that. At a 75% loan to value, my cash on cash returns were over 12%, a figure we could get excited about.

However, if I did not assume the loan, there was still defeasance (like a pre-payment penalty) to deal with. My attorney said it would cost more than $280,000 to put a new loan on it. The seller had no intention of paying it, and if I added that to the cash I raised, it really knocked my cash on cash returns below what I felt I could offer and raise. I certainly did not want to pay it out of my pocket.

I had to figure something out because the clock was ticking. Only 54 more days to go.

Chapter 7
The Art of the Deal

"As long as you are going to be thinking anyway, think big."
~ Donald Trump

Next on the path of self-storage acquisition are the negotiations with the current owner and the contract. I am not an expert in this area, and there are a lot of resources better than this out there to assist you in negotiating strategies. I can just share my experience, what I have done right and what I have done wrong. The old adage of "buy low, sell high" always works, but with self-storage this is easier said than done.

This type of real estate has the lowest foreclosure rate of any kind. There are not too many distressed self-storage facilities. One has to look far and wide to find those we can "buy low". I am not saying it cannot happen; I am just saying I do not run into them very often.

This makes the analysis and the negotiation factor that much more important when buying self-storage.

In my formative business development, a book by Stephen Covey was popularly titled *The Seven Habits of Highly Effective People*. Everyone has a book that shaped them professionally, and this was one of them for me. In fact, I could overlay my entire self-storage business inside the context of this book—even the name we use. (Q2 Self-Storage stands for quadrant 2 activity, which is what building the self-storage business is for us).

Why this book is important in this chapter is because in the background of all my dealings with the seller, or the seller's agent, is the concept of win-win. I know, especially with self-storage, I am not going to get what I want, unless the seller is going to get what he wants. So I am always listening for that. It took me a long time to learn, but if you are listening for something, you will always hear it.

The days of the sacristy mindset are not completely over, but it is becoming less and less effective. A belief in sacristy creates a win-ner-take-all mentality. This belief system, or context of negotiating from, makes winners and losers in any negotiations. I cannot win unless you lose, or vice versa. It comes from a deep-seated belief that the universe holds a limited amount of good and that, in order for me to have mine, you cannot have yours. Few will say this is their belief, but many act and think from it. If you really want to know what your deep-seated beliefs are, look at your actions in how you negotiate with anyone. Your actions speak louder than what you say, even to yourself.

So I have to create a transaction where I get what I want, and the seller gets what he wants. This is one reason a business plan is critical. For example, I know exactly what makes a "good" deal for me. I then look at how I can create that, and give the seller what he wants. For example, I am negotiating now for a facility and I want the following:

- The ability to pay a 12% cash on cash return on the equity for the first five years, then to be able to refinance the property and give the investors their investment back within the first five years.

That is a win for me now in the execution of my business plan. So this is what I am currently looking for. I then listen for what the seller wants. If I cannot figure it out exactly, no problem. I will know soon enough after I submit a LOI or contract. I usually know at least some of what it is prior to writing offers, but I will soon find out all. In general these are the steps to go through:

1. **Find** property and tour.
2. **Preliminary** analysis.
3. **Write** letter of intent (LOI).
4. **Write** contract.

5. **Complete** due diligence.
6. **Close** on self-storage facility.

Letter of Intent (LOI)

I do not always move through these steps exactly, but in general that is it. Sometimes I skip the LOI and go straight to contract, for example. I usually like writing the LOI because it is from there I will get what the seller really wants. In the LOI, we are discussing the basic business terms of a transaction: the price, the length of the due diligence period, what data I expect from them to complete my analysis, and by when I will get it. I like this step because the seller can focus on the basic terms of a transaction, not all of the legal stuff in a full contract. An LOI is easier to say yes to. One generally has to get a lot of *yes* before a closing takes place. It also allows you to find out exactly what is important and has to happen for the seller to close. If there is some very tricky issue, it also gives you time. You can get a yes, then deal with tricky issues in the contract. Issues could be owners giving up all rights to a name of the site domain, proving their sign is in compliance, etc. Those types of things (that could potentially upset a seller) can be dealt with after he feels like he has a deal with you.

Also, you can generally write the LOI without incurring any legal expense. After you get an accepted LOI, then if you are going to use a lawyer—and I recommend using a lawyer—you can give them the LOI and say, "Create a contract." You are only incurring legal expense because you have a yes on a deal.

The website **www.CreatingWealthThroughSelfStorage.com** has sample letters of intent. I do not put sample contracts on the site because I am not a lawyer and I do not want to be practicing law by offering them to you.

The Contract

Purchasing a self-storage facility is different from purchasing most other types of real estate. In essence, you are purchasing (1) a piece of real estate and (2) an ongoing business. Shopping centers, apartments, office buildings, and most every other kind of investment real estate do not have the second component. That is why this is a unique transaction and I recommend getting expert legal help.

Here are some items that have to be addressed in a contract.

- *Actual buyer and seller:*   Make sure you have the names exactly correct to make sure it is an enforceable contract.
- *What you are purchasing:* You are purchasing all the real estate, the fixtures, *and* the business, including all the equipment that makes a business run (i.e., computers, tools, golf carts, etc.). You will need a legal description somewhere in the contact.
- *Price, terms, and good faith deposit.*
- *Contingencies:*   I try to have as few as possible, but have them as broad as possible.
    - o   I usually have one contingency that includes inspections of the physical property, the business records, and an environmental report if required by the bank.
    - o   I usually have a contingency of the buyer approving a feasibility report that the buyer orders and pays for.
    - o   I may or may not have it contingent upon financing. If I am in a large market competing with REITS, I may leave this out but have the other contingencies broad enough to be able to get out of the contract if I need to. On your first few contracts, I would leave in a financing contingency until you have some comfort level with how the process works.
    - o   I try to have this "due diligence period" be as long as possible, while the seller usually wants it as short as possible. I have gone as short as 45 days, and often have to buy an extension with part of the good-faith

deposit becoming non-refundable, and as long as 120 days. It is usually around 60 days.

- *Non-compete*:   I usually have some kind of non-compete clause in the contract that prohibits the seller from entering back in to the sub-market where the facility is located.

- *Some kind of clause that if the financial condition of the property substantively changes after contract but before closing, the buyer can terminate the contract.*

- *All the standard closing items, such as tax prorations, etc.*

- *Some clause indicating the buyer is also purchasing all the "intellectual property" such as the name, website domains, signs, etc.* If it is a large company or REIT, this clause usually will not work, but for smaller facilities it can save you a lot of headaches. Even if you are changing the name, have some clause like this in the contract.

- *I always make sure there is some clause in the contract that deals with the past due rent and uncollected rent.* On the day of closing, I make sure all uncollected rent is the buyer's. If there is no clause like this in the contract, I have seen where the uncollected rent in the 30-day past due column is prorated between buyer and seller. It should be the buyer's, because the buyer has to collect it and there is no guarantee they will.

- *All the other standard clauses attorneys love to put into contracts. Look for their representations and warranties and make sure they do UCC searches on the current owner and company you are buying.* (UCC stands for Uniform Commercial Code. This is a database including tax lien and debtor searches, pending lawsuits and more).

Remember: You are purchasing a business as well as real estate. Have a lawyer you like and can work with who understands self-storage, and have a contract evolve that you have confidence in.

After an LOI is agreed to by both parties, get the contract to the seller as soon as possible. I always try to be the one who generates the contract so it is my contract form. Sometimes the seller will counter on another form. I don't make a big deal of it, but if possible, I will use mine.

My relationship to this period is *I am trying to get the facility standing still for a known period of time at a known price*, so I control it, and can take the time necessary to analyze completely and make sure there are no surprises. If the financial analysis from The Valuator software still allows me to meet my goals after I replace assumptions with real numbers from the due diligence period, we purchase it. If not, we let it go. Either way, if this period is executed correctly, it is up to **us** to decide. I like that.

Chapter 8
APPLICATION: The Other Side of the Art of the Deal

"Sometimes your best investments are the ones you don't make."
~ Donald Trump

I was moving fast toward getting the facility under contract. Due to the fact that this property had a land lease and a CMB (commercial mortgage backed) mortgage assumption, I hired an attorney to draft the contract. It took almost three weeks. When I received the contract back for review, I set an appointment with both owners (the "money" partner and "managing" partner).

If I was raising in cash the difference between the loan assumption with a loan balance of $2 million and the sales price of $6.5 million; the $4.5 million equity was only going to generate 8% cash on cash return with their previous year's income and *our* projected expenses. I have to do better than that to get the attention of the investors I work with. I thought the "money" partner would realize that, because I am sure he had been in my position before. I ran the scenario in the Valuator with them holding a second mortgage up to the 75% loan to value, and—presto—the magic cash on cash return was hit.

At that meeting, just as I thought, the "money" partner got it; the "managing" partner thought that was my problem, not his. Fortunately for me, the "money" partner (as in most cases money partners do), won out. I got the property under contract with the second mortgage, and the due diligence period began. I was able to secure an owner-held second mortgage for the duration of the first mortgage, and would pay them both when the first was up and I could refinance the facility.

In a few chapters we'll explore the due diligence of this property, but here I want to focus on contracts and negotiations. I was receiving from the seller all the due diligence materials I was asking for. Part of my due diligence was using the attorney I had hired to work with the existing lender and coach me through this "big boy" loan assumption. I had never done anything like this before.

This was not just any loan assumption; it was not like assuming a loan at a bank. This loan was packaged with millions of dollars' worth of other loans, and sold to some retirement fund in Europe, it turned out. To modify the terms of this loan was a big deal. It was also very expensive. The assumption fee alone was $28,000 dollars. The process of getting qualified to assume it was no small task, either. I have assembled a core group of common members (not investors, a group that qualifies for the loan) who had some strong financial strength (see the chapter on our LLC organization), but this was going to be a very difficult task. Finally, after I jumped through all my hoops and spent all the money, I had the privilege of assuming a 5.5% loan for five more years that would be very hard to sell and impossible to refinance before then. Only a yahoo like me would put a deal like this under contract.

The deeper I got into this loan assumption during the due diligence, the more I realized that not only did I not want to assume the loan, but we probably were not going to be able to, anyway. The legal cost and assumption fees to me to assume were in excess of $50,000. However, if I did not assume the loan, to pay it off the defeasance was $286,000 to the seller. I did not want that loan, but I did not see the seller spending $286,000 for the privilege to sell this facility that was doing very well. What to do?

I was getting more discouraged every day. In the morning, I use the first hour of my day to meditate. I would use that time to "visualize" my owning the facility, and every morning I *did* see my group getting it, but at night I was scared and very concerned about assuming that loan. During the day I just plowed ahead.

This was in the last quarter of 2012 and the presidential election was during that time. In our meetings, I had heard different comments from the sellers about their disdain for our president. I do not want this book to be political, and I am sure I will turn away more than 50% of readers if I discussed my rather liberal political views, so I won't. But these guys had no problem discussing theirs. As in most of the business world I traffic in, I just nodded my head and smiled as they talked politics. But there was a real concern on their part that things "would go to hell if he is re-elected."

One night I was watching the television, worried about how much money I had sunk into the deal and knowing I was most likely not going to be able to close because of the loan assumption. Actually, I was less worried about the money than I was of what my partners would think of me—going that far and having to pull the plug on what could have been determined very early on in the deal (and many thousands of dollars ago). And they would have been right. That was my mind-set as I watched one of the presidential debates. I cannot remember which one it was, but President Obama really came out on top. Even the conservative pundits at FOX said so.

Then it hit me: That was it! That was my ticket out of that loan assumption.

I pulled out my computer, opened up the Valuator, and put in a new loan at 4.5% interest (the current interest rate of the day). With a new loan I was going to be paying $50,000-plus less in interest the first year than with the two mortgages I would have under the present contract. I knew I had to get the right to put a new loan on the property. The next morning I called the "money" partner and asked him what he thought of the debate. He had his opinion. I suggested he call his accountant because, "it might be better to consider—just consider; I am not pushing, but it may be more advantageous to you—to pay the defeasance now, and perhaps I could help with the cost, than to pay what will surely be much higher capital gains tax rates if Obama wins." There was a long silence on the phone and then he said I may be right. I said I would be willing to throw the cost of the assumption I was going to be paying anyway for the defeasance.

After a few days and three conversations, we modified the contract to allow me to put a new loan on the deal and pay $50,000 toward the defeasance cost. I was going to place a new 75% loan to value loan at 4.5% on the property and the seller was paying the defeasance to lock in the 2012 capital gains tax rate because Obama could very well win.

A win-win? Well, this was not my proudest moment. There will be times in your career where you will wonder if you did the right thing. I still do not know. I still have a good relationship with the sellers, and the "money" partner is very savvy and one of the toughest negotiators I have ever seen. They have both done better (if you measure in net worth) than I have. But to be truthful, there are nights where I wondered if I played on their fears to get what I wanted. They were definitely afraid of Obama winning the election, and I used that to my advantage. Everyone has their own values and beliefs through which decisions are filtered. Sometimes under pressure and with a lot at stake, decisions come out a particular way. In this case, this is how it came out.

We were moving toward a December 31, 2012, closing, and I had to hustle to get a new first mortgage on the property and raise the $1,625,000 equity. I had about six weeks left to do it all. What *a problem*. But I was smiling every morning as I began solving this new problem. This was a problem I was very excited to have.

Chapter 9
The Due Diligence Period

"Do not focus only on your needs; focus on your purpose."
~ Deborah Brodie

Y ou have a property standing still now for a known price and a known period of time (under contract). Now what? There are five main spaces to move through in my opinion.

1. The financial inspection of the books and records, and property information
2. The physical property inspections
3. The loan application, underwriting, and approval process
4. The feasibility report
5. Organizational formation

These are the steps I go through. Usually, we end up working on all of them simultaneously, but I try to be clear which area I am working on and what needs to happen in each area.

Financial Inspection and Property Information

Below are items I get from the seller. I write a letter within 24 hours of the property going under contract requesting these items, even though my contract usually references these items and the length of time the seller has to get them to me. If they are delayed in getting to me, there is usually a clause in the contract that adjusts the due diligence time period accordingly. (You can find a sample copy of the due diligence letter at **www.CreatingWealthThroughSelfStorage.com**)

- Copy of insurance policies
- Survey
- Title policy (if you have from last loan)
- Phase I environmental study
- Current rent roll (We will update the day before closing.)
- Copies of last three years federal and state tax returns (for lender)
- Copy of tax bills
- Service contracts
- Bank statements (last three years)
- Utility bills
- Monthly closes from operating system for year to date and past three years
- Architectural drawings or building plans
- Capital expenditures (detailed of last three years, current and planned)
- Profit and loss statements for the last three years (end of year) with closing balance sheet, and monthly profit and loss for year to date with month end balance sheets

If you can get all of this, you really have everything you need. I spend most of my time taking the data of the P&Ls (profit and loss statements) and updating the financial analysis in the Valuator. I usually start with operating expenses and alter the utilities, maintenance, and other expenses with actuals. I use the tax bill to come up with a tax rate and modify the property tax number under the operating expenses. I look for how much they have been spending in capital expenses. I will be able to tell how accurate my assumptions were about the expenses.

I study the service contracts to see which ones, if any, I will have to assume. I then alter the Valuator accordingly. Lastly, I turn over survey, title commitment, phase I environmental, etc. to my attorney and where I have applied for a loan, so they can do their inspections of the documents to make sure those aspects of the deal is in place.

Physical Property Inspections

I usually pay a builder to physically inspect the facility. It took me a while to figure out how to get the physical inspection done in an accurate and efficient manner. The usual "home inspectors" were inadequate for this type of inspection. (I found this out the hard way brokering a deal for a client who later got mad at me for suggesting this route). In the beginning of my self-storage career, I used a contractor I had a relationship with, but there were certain aspects of self-storage construction they missed. I finally settled on the contractor we use when we build or expand and add new self-storage. They do a good job. The inspections usually cost us between $1,000 and $2,500, depending on size and location of facility (travel time). These guys know what to look for.

They almost always find something. I then ask them to give me a bid on the repair work. The bid breaks down exactly where and what work is to be done to bring the physical property up to our standards. Usually I have my crew do the work they specified in their bids, but from those bids I have a number to put (either theirs or mine from their bid) in the "first year's expenses" in the Valuator.

I have found some real issues before in the physical inspections. Once the inspector found some of the buildings had slipped off their foundation. I have seen roofs that were not long enough and created real water issues. On buildings where the doors face north, I know if there are cold winters, that side will not get much sun, and I am going to have ice blocking the doors if there are no, or undersized, gutters. You learn more than you think you will know after a number of these inspections.

Finding issues in the inspections does not bother me. I am looking for what I have to spend to get the facility up to our business plan's standards. I am just looking for a number. If after putting that number in, I can still hit the cash on cash returns that currently drives our acquisition decisions, I purchase. If I cannot, I either get the deal at a price that does or I terminate the transaction.

The Loan

Very early in the due diligence time period I recommend applying for the loan. There are four basic loan providers you can use in this business:

1. Local banks or credit unions
2. Local banks that can offer government guarantees for a portion of lenders loan (i.e., SBA [Small Business Administration] loan)
3. Life insurance loans
4. CMB (commercial mortgage backed) conduit loans

Local banks get the bulk of self-storage loans from people starting in the business. We have a lot of loans on self-storage through local and regional banks. The advantage is that you usually already have a relationship with a bank or can develop one fairly easily. Unless it is a big institution, it will most likely be making its decisions locally. In other words, there are a bunch of people (usually men) sitting around a table talking about you and your loan. I find it is easier to influence them positively by putting together a strong "loan request proposal". I actually put a binder together with the following information:

- A one- to two-page written executive summary, summarizing our plans for the facility (i.e., we are going to upgrade and expand the property, or we are going to give it a face lift and replace the manager, etc.)
- My financial analysis
- Sellers or seller's agents marketing package
- The feasibility report when completed (Usually I apply for the loan about the time I am ordering the feasibility report. I leave a section in the binder with a sheet inserted that says "Feasibility report to be inserted here.")
- Contract and supporting documents
- Financial history of property received from seller in the due diligence information
- Financial information of the people who will be guaranteeing the loan

- Summary of my experience with the industry (If you are in the beginning stages of the business, include information on your partners' experience, the management company you are using, or your past experience with other property types that offers the type of experience that will be useful in running a self-storage facility).

When I show up to the meeting with a banker, this has already been put together. This (1) speeds up the process, and (2) lets the loan officer know that we know (or at least appear to know) what we are doing. In my experience, most lenders would rather lend to someone they have confidence in and less on the property, than a great property in the hands of someone they have little confidence in.

As I start getting term sheets (letters from the banks indicating the loans terms they are willing to offer us), I modify the financial analysis to reflect those terms. My goal is to move as fast as possible to get a loan we can say yes to, and have the loan officer take that to the committee (the guys sitting around the table) and get approval subject to an appraisal and environmental reports.

The negative of these types of loans are:

- They can be arbitrary. What happens depends on how the guys around the table feel the day your loan comes up. They could also have other loans on self-storage, and they feel their bank is over-extended in that property type.
- You will have to personally guarantee the loan. If I think the facility is being purchased right, I will guarantee the loan. In my opinion, if you are bullish on the deal and not willing to guarantee a loan, you are sending mixed messages to the lender and your partners. But at some point, because I am on so many loans, the banks will begin to have issues with the amount I am guaranteeing. There are only so many loans one can guarantee and still get more loans.

SBA

It was not too long ago that SBA (Small Business Administration) loans did not cover self-storage. Some lenders used to have a hard time with self-storage, calling it a "special use" product, and would not lend. The thinking was that if they had to take it back in a foreclosure, they could only sell it as self-storage, thus limiting the market and their ability to sell. When the recession hit in 2008 and all types of commercial real estate began to be foreclosed on, lenders noticed that self-storage had a very small foreclosure rate. (The last figure I saw was 3.46% of all self-storage facilities are foreclosed on. That is almost 10% less than most other kinds of commercial real estate).

In 2010, the SBA told lenders they would start offering their guarantee to self-storage operators. I remember thinking this was a big deal because local banks would realize what a good risk lending on self-storage was. It has been a long time since I have heard the "special use" argument from a lender.

Basically, if a lender is approved to underwrite an SBA loan, the lender has up to 60% of the loan guaranteed by the Small Business Administration, thus reducing the bank's risk and theoretically allowing loans to happen that otherwise would not, thus allowing a business to be created that may not without the government assistance.

I am not an expert on SBA loans, and have never personally used one, but there are a lot of people who do know about them, and these loans can make the difference. A layman might look at it like an FHA loan from commercial users. This is not the place to go into details about SBA loans, but in general a borrower has to qualify through the bank, and then the borrower and project have to qualify with SBA. The bank decides if the borrowers are credit worthy, and the SBA makes sure the borrowers and the property meet their guidelines to qualify for their guarantee. If so, a buyer can go in with as little as 10% equity and have a self-amortizing loan, which is sometimes up to 25 years.

There are more loan costs (which are usually rolled up into the loan) and more paperwork and qualification, and it takes a longer time to be approved, but all in all, SBA is a very good option for many buyers.

Find a bank or commercial mortgage broker that specializes in

SBA and does a lot of them. It is not a fun process, but it could make the difference between someone getting in the business or not.

Life Insurance Loans

Most likely, if you are not an experienced commercial real estate investor, a life insurance loan will not be what you use to acquire your first self-storage facility. However, they can be a great source as you grow.

Generally (and I mean very generally), insurance companies use commercial loans as a way of getting a return on the premiums they collect. They have strict guidelines, such as a $2 million minimum loan amount in most cases, borrowers have to qualify and be high net worth, the real estate has to be "institutional grade" in most cases, and their loan to value (LTV) is usually 65% or less (thus a borrower has to come up with at least a 35% down payment).

The advantage is, if you jump through the hoops and obtain a life insurance loan, in most cases you do not have to personally guarantee the loan. They will look to the property alone to secure the loan. This becomes more and more important as you grow your portfolio. Without these types of loans, there may be a time where it becomes very hard to qualify for more personally guaranteed loans.

Commercial mortgage brokers or larger banks can place these for you, and there is usually a cost. For our business plan, we are often expanding, upgrading, or even building from ground up to create some value, and these loans will not work with those scenarios. However, when we have it stabilized and with a history of 85% stabilized occupancy or better, and it is time to refinance, these are the loans we seek, because we have the time and the long-term benefits of having non-recourse debt on the project.

Explore and talk with some commercial mortgage loan officers to determine how this type of loan may fit into your business strategy.

CMB (Commercial Mortgage Backed) Loans

Somewhat similar to life insurance loans, these are institutional-grade loans that are designed for institutional-grade real estate and for strong buyers. In general, these loans are packaged together with other CMB loans and sold as investment instruments on Wall Street. The buyers of those instruments get the interest from these notes as a return on their investment.

Usually, the property is institutional grade, the LTV is 65%, and the buyers have strong financial strength. As with insurance loans, the property alone is the security for the note. These loans are generally 20-year amortizations with the loan in place for 10 years. If you try to pay it off, there is a large cost to do so called defeasance. Defeasance is the cost of putting another institutional-grade investment instrument in lieu of the loan, generating the same return as the paid-off loan did for the buyer of the loan package sold on Wall Street. It is expensive, not fun, and very time consuming to do so. I have been through it more than once trying to put a deal together with one of these loans on a property. Do not get these loans unless you are sure you are going to hold the property for a long time. To sell it, the buyers would have to qualify for an assumption and would have to have the difference between the sales price of the self-storage facility and the loan balance in cash. Most of the time, there is a prohibition of a second mortgage for what is usually a large gap between sales price and the loan balance.

These loans are non-recourse to the borrower (except for certain situations such as fraud) and, again, allow certain types of individuals or institutions to grow a portfolio without having to personally guarantee all the loans they have secured.

If you remain in the business for some time, a mortgage broker will bring this type of loan up as an option. Listen closely to determine if these loans are right for you and where you are.

Put your loan proposal request together, and hit three or more lenders that meet your needs and are appropriate to the facility you have under contract.

Feasibility Report

At the same time you are ordering your inspections, putting your loan proposal request together, *order a feasibility report*. I never buy a facility without the feasibility report. They have saved my tail on more than one occasion. Do not think, "Well, I know this market" and not order one. There could be someone who has pulled a permit to build next door and you know nothing about it.

> We built Louisville, Kentucky's first urban 100% self-storage facility. Many people, including our partnership, had no idea how deep the market really was, being on the edge of the downtown business district of the city and building a facility that had multi-floors. The first thing we did was order a feasibility report. The report indicated there was a 103,000-square-foot shortfall between supply and demand for this area. We were only building out 60,000 square feet in three phases. Because of this report, the bank as well as the partners felt very safe taking the risk of being the first to do something in our market.

A feasibility report quantifies the supply/demand for self-storage in the sub-market the facility is located. It is done by an independent third party, so banks and investors will accept their findings (whereas they may question the findings if you or someone else involved in the transaction is coming up with the results).

In short, those who complete feasibility reports will determine what the market for that facility is. Once they have the market, they will look at the population in that market. They then have data that will tell them how many square feet of self-storage per person that market uses (from the Self Storage Association). Then they look at the current supply (your competition) to see how many square feet of self-storage are serving the area, what the sizes are, and what the occupancy rates are. Next they can calculate if there is over-supply for the sub-market (too many units for the population) or under-supply (not enough for the population). The report we had completed in the Houston, Texas, market indicated there was a 326,000-square-foot potential demand with only 123,000 square feet supplying it. Would you feel safe buying a facility in that market and adding 26,000 square feet more of units? We sure did. So did the bank.

Feasibility reports also look at what that market is renting in unit sizes, how fast new facilities were rented, the best unit mix, and even some best practices you may put in the facility you are considering based on what the competition is doing. People completing feasibility reports will also check to see if any projects are pending or have received approval. I once had a piece of land under contract to build a facility, and the person completing the feasibility report told me, "You have a great site. You just have one problem: Someone has pulled a permit and next month starts construction on a 100,000-square-foot facility less than one mile from you. You do not want to be 10 months behind that guy." I let the site go. (We ended up buying the facility he referred to in his feasibility report 10 years later). If I had not completed the feasibility report, I most likely would not be in the business today.

You are going to spend a lot of money on a facility. Don't cheap out and try to save a few thousand dollars by not getting the feasibility report. Get it! You can find people who specialize in self-storage in your market, and there are national providers of this service easily found through the associations.

Organizational Structure

You will have to determine how you are going to own the facility. Usually, your lawyer and accountant will give you lots of advice on how to do this and what is best for your situation.

Most of the time people own self-storage facilities, or any income producing real estate asset, with single asset limited liability companies or S Corporations. This limits your liability. If you are sued for something that happens on that facility, the only asset in the company is that one facility and they cannot get to your other assets, like your house or personal bank accounts.

You do not have to have this fully figured out at the time you write the contract, but you will by the time you close. I usually write the contract in the name of a company I am the sole owner in. Then before closing, I assign the contract to a newly formed LLC (limited liability company) that has been formed by our attorney for owning this facility.

Due Diligence Period

You will usually have 30 to 60 days in today's market to complete all of the above. It is a race, but it is a race you can win. Remember: You are in the business now of creating good problems for yourself. Lay it out on paper, check items off as you go, and be aware of what is not completed yet.

There are a few more items not listed here that your attorney will need to handle. There are also items the closing company or closing attorney will need to take care of, such as title work (checking to make sure there are no problems in the chain of ownership) and UCC searches (making sure the company that currently owns the facility you are buying has no pending legal problems you may be also buying with the facility). I will let them advise you of that because I do not want to be practicing law in this book and hear from any of them.

In general, during this period, I am altering the financial analysis, replacing assumptions with accurate data, and making sure there are not other problems I do not know about. How much will I need to really spend to get the facility to where I want it? What are the real expenses the current owner pays that I will have to pay? How full is my competition? How good are they? What will my real loan be?

Once I have the Valuator financial analysis where I think all the facts are in, I look at it. For us it is simple. I am looking for a couple of things based on our goals and business plan: What is the cash on cash return in the first five years, and can I create enough equity to refinance in the first five years and pay back my investors?

Then I either pull the trigger and close, or I let it go.

Chapter 10
The Unfolding

"Our truest life is when we are in dreams awake."
~ Henry David Thoreau

Most people's relationship with language is weak—very weak. In fact, most people rarely, if ever, think about language. However, it is the water we swim in. Our entire reality is perceived through language (at least most of the conscious part of our reality). Human beings are the only animal we know of that perceives reality through language. Something happens (a stimulus) and we interpret it through language. For a human being, language—the spoken word—is almost everything.

"In the beginning, there was the word."

However, most of us have a very weak relationship with the spoken word. If pressed, most people would say something like "I use language to describe what is happening in the world and in my mind". In other words, language is a descriptive tool. It is, but that is a very weak use of the spoken word.

What if for you language was a creative force? What if you could create with language?

In 2010, I was in another workshop for entrepreneurs, but this was unlike any workshop I had ever been in. I had purchased the self-storage facility that got me back into the self-storage business (see the Case Study) and I was developing one in Louisville's urban core (Louisville's first urban self-storage). I was really extended financially. I had been through an 18-month period of earning no income from my commercial real estate practice, and my wife, feeling scared, had gone back to work from her early retirement. I was doing better than many people I knew, but if you were using language to describe my situation, it would have been more like the previous sentence: no income coming in.

I created a "$60,000,000 Self-Storage Portfolio" in that workshop. If I had to look into the future, and if I got to say what that future was, why not create a future worthy of a career or a professional life? I was tired of feeling like a victim of the recession. I realized I could either drift through the recession and most likely survive financially, then slowly replace my savings. I had depleted my savings, and it would take a long time to replace the $200,000 or so I had spent of it living with no income and developing this second facility. I would do okay, but this was most likely it as far as self-storage for a few more years until I replenished my savings.

Or, I could use language to create a much more exciting future to live. I chose the latter. I think the exercise was something like "If you knew you could win at anything professionally, what would you do with the next five years of your professional life?" That was the beginning of my second career as a self-storage professional. I loved the business, and I created a future called "60,000,000 Self-Storage Portfolio".

New Problem

Now I had a real problem. I had no more money to develop that future. However, I know that if one speaks a future into existence, and then completely puts one's entire focus, energy, and belief into that future, it has to unfold. It may not always be pretty, but it will happen.

At that time I joined a networking group of business owners to tap into each other's skill base and refer our client base to each other's. I had hated networking groups in the past and found them a total waste of my time, but this group seemed different. I was invited in because of my commercial real estate experience, and I immediately realized the strength and power of the group assembled. For the most part they all owned their companies and had an abundance of experience in their respective disciplines.

There was an attorney who went out on his own who had helped a local, publicly traded restaurant do its early expansion. In a meeting, he explained to me the way they formed their LLCs for each restaurant in a way that allowed the owners of the restaurant brand to expand using other people's money before they were publicly traded. What a huge resource. Within in a month of creating the future called "60,000,000 Self-Storage Portfolio", I had a structure that appeared to allow me to fulfill that future.

I firmly believe—no, I know—that if you create something in language, and then every day put your energy into it and stay present, your path will unfold. I had to be able to be present enough to hear that I should have the meeting with the attorney. I also had to be able to hear what he was saying, filtered through a future I was very present to. It was not that difficult and is available for everybody.

New Organizational Structure

Our new organizational structure is actually very simple: I would form an LLC for each facility. The LLC would be made up of two kinds of members. All are "common members". However, some of the common members have "preferred" status until they get their money back with a negotiated return. As soon as I heard this, I thought about all the financial analyses I had run on self-storage facilities. I realized in the self-storage deals I had done so far, in most cases, created enough equity in five years to refinance and pay back anyone who invested the equity. I re-ran the financial analysis on projects I had sold or owned, and used this new formula. In most cases, it worked.

So here is how it works in our storage business. There is a core group of common investors (I am one of them) who find the deals, put the deals together, guarantee the loans, oversees the day-to-day management and asset management, and executes the strategy for that facility (i.e., build the expansion, re-position the facility, etc.). Then there are the investors. They put the money in the deal, they have no risk other than the money they invest, and they do not guarantee the loans. The investors just receive a return on their investment until they get all their money back. Then their "preferred" status goes away, and they can stay in at the lower percentage of ownership or be bought out by the common members, whichever they want.

Our facilities each have a separate LLC. The common member core group owns 70% of the LLC and the investors own 30%. We are all common members. However, the investors have preferred status until they get all their money back. The event of them getting their money back is called a "conversion". Before the conversion, they have "preferred" rights. They get 90% of the cash flow. Also, before their money is all returned, it takes unanimous consent of all the members for certain things to happen (in other words, they have a lot of say over the deal until they get their money back). For example, it takes unanimous consent for any other loans go on the property, if their shares are diluted (i.e., if more money comes in the deal or new partners come in the deal, etc.). They have a lot of rights and power that go away after they get all their money back with the pre-determined return. In most cases, we offer them 12% cash on cash return each year until we can cause the conversion. The conversion happens when I can refinance the property, and pay the preferred members their investment back plus any shortfall that may be there from the yearly cash on cash return of the 12% they are due.

If we are buying a stabilized property (like the one we have been discussing in this book in the APPLICATION chapter titles), they will start getting their 12% return from the first month after closing. If it is a project where we are expanding the property, and only after the expansion is stabilized is there enough money to start paying the 12% return, their 12% is carried forward. Any part of that 12% per year that has not been paid is due at the time of the conversion.

Within five minutes of being in the conversation with the attorney who was a member of the networking group, I saw this LLC formation clearly. I knew it could work.

So I, in theory, had a way I could see to use other people's money to create the future I have created. I still had some "problems" to solve. I love these types of problems. I get energy from these kinds of problems. I live for these problems.

I was not strong enough financially to be the guarantor on these loans, and I did not know enough people with lots of money to invest. You can't advertise for these investors. But as soon as I heard the formation structure from the attorney and saw it could work, I knew I could solve the other two problems.

The first big issue was: How could I guarantee the loans so that the investors did not have to? If I am not strong enough financially, I need a core group who is.

Over the years, I had developed a reputation for being an "expert" in self-storage. I had some credibility. So when I approached people who knew me, they had some confidence I knew what I was talking about. Growing a portfolio of self-storage was new to me, and in reality I was into a space I have never been, but that is what being an entrepreneur is all about.

I thought about all the people I know, and within less than a minute I knew who I was going to approach. I had a friend with whom I had previously worked professionally and for whom I had the utmost respect. We actually owned the property management company I referenced before where we managed office space for my client base. He had gone on and had another partnership that had become one of the largest developers in the nation of low-income senior housing. He realized how to take something that worked and do it over and over, and he had done very well. I knew from talking to him that, although he owned a lot of real estate, as a developer of the product, he was making most of his money as a developer. He had third-party management in place (so he was not making all of the management fees) and the deals were syndicated on Wall Street, so those investors "owned" most of the projects. I figured (still am not totally sure) that my friend was getting most of his current income from development fees. What if I could offer him a way to have significant cash flow in the future, with no energy spent today (I would expend the energy)? All he had to do was help me guarantee the loans until the conversion.

After the conversion, the majority of the cash flow reverts to the common members of the LLC. In other words, after the investors get their money back, the common core group will be getting 70% of the cash flow of the project. I approached my friend with my plan.

He and his partner agreed to try it on a project with me to see how it would work. This is no small thing. To have someone's trust and to sign their name to a loan where conceivably they could be required to pay back millions of dollars if the deal goes south, that is a big deal. There needs to be a lot of trust. But apparently it was there. I truly believe the trust they have in me is a sacred oath I have to respect. I will do anything to protect their positions in the deals because of the trust they have placed in me. If you feel that way, it will show, and I don't think you have to say it often. Just be it.

Most of the structure was in place. I now had the ability to get a loan; what was still missing was the equity. I began approaching people I knew. One of my first calls was to a person I had hired before in my first incarnation of self-storage. She had been in charge of managing the facility managers and, since we were bought out, she had married into a family that owned a self-storage facility. She and her husband said they knew lots of people who would like to invest and they could help me grow the company and be assets in the day-to-day operational management.

I instantly knew she and her husband were the other missing piece for me in the core group. They knew a lot of people, and they could help manage the property. Facility managers need an owner who is always focused on them, and if I am growing the portfolio, I cannot be that person. Maria and Scott are much better at that than I am, anyway.

I had developed a core group of people that filled in the gaps. I had: financial strength for loans, access to people who want to invest, and the ability to handle day-to-day operational matters. I had the plan, vision, and ability to find properties, analyze, and structure deals so that they would close. The core group was in place: The financially strong friend and his partner would own 50% of the core group (money always talks), I would own 25%, and the operational husband and wife who would bring in the money and help with operations would own 25%. Together the group would own 70% of a deal and the investors would own 30%.

That is our general structure. It can vary. For example, if a deal cannot spin off 12%, we may increase the investors' ownership to 35% or something to compensate on the back side for smaller cash on cash returns.

The structure was in place, so we just needed a deal. Within a month, the deal came in. I have been writing about it throughout the book in the APPLICATION chapters. We were moving toward a December 31, 2012, closing, and I had to hustle to get a new first mortgage on the property and raise the $1,625,000 equity. I had about six weeks left to do it all.

Chapter 11
APPLICATION: The Close

"Imagination is more important than knowledge."
~ Albert Einstein

I could now get a new first mortgage and within three hours I had put together the loan request proposal. I had to move quickly, so a life insurance loan was out of the question. I went to a local bank that had loaned on a previous self-storage project, and someone with whom I already had a relationship. He indicated it would be tight, but he felt they could close within the 12/31/12 deadline. (We had to close within the year to lock in the 2012 capital gains rates for the seller).

Initially I had requested a 75% loan to value loan. That afternoon, my new core partners had me presenting a package to their world of friends and members of an investment group they were in.

I also called a builder I had used to construct a facility and had them do the physical inspection. Within three days I had everything moving forward, and I spent the next few weeks presenting the deal to potential investors. Within two weeks I had commitments for the 25% equity. I was offering a 12% cash on cash return on their money, and within five years we could give them all their equity back, at which point they could stay in the deal, or raise their hand and say, "Buy me out" at that value in five years. We had a very investor-friendly deal structured.

The lead investors spent a lot of time going through the LLC documents, and making requests to change them and grant even more protection to the investors. I really had no problem with it and my relationship to this process was that I was creating a boilerplate document that could be used over and over. If *these* lead investors would like it, anyone would. They knew what they were doing.

The appraisal came in, the bank took the loan to committee, and all was right with the world. Then I got the call from the loan officer.

He asked if I wanted the good news or bad news first. By now you should know I said the good. We were approved. The bad? I was approved for a 65% loan, not 75% loan to value. We had to close within a week.

"No problem," I said to the loan officer. I hung up the phone and slumped down. How was I going to raise the balance—another $350,000, — go through all the paces an investor or investors go through, and then close in a few days? These investors had more than a month of going back and forth, asking questions, and having their lawyers and accountants review, advise, and set up the structures through which they would invest. Less than a week seemed out of the question, and it was.

Then my eyes rested on a sign complaint that had arrived via fax earlier that week. The seller (the "managing" member of the group selling the facility to us) had faxed over a complaint someone had filed on the size of our sign.

So I did what I had done before. I went to the seller. I told the "money" partner what had happened. My attorney had created a document indicating the seller was to handle this complaint and resolve it after the closing. They would have to pay for any sign that may need to be replaced if it was ruled against us. My attorney advised that odds were we would keep the sign. It was just a competitor who was angry he/she could not get the same size sign filing the complaint. Ours had been up for more than 10 years.

I asked the "money" partner if they would hold a second mortgage for 90 days while I raised the additional 10% equity and the sign issue was resolved. If he could do that, we were ready to close. I said our core group would guarantee the second to him. He agreed.

My last hurdle was overcome. The bank agreed to the short-term second. We closed.

This was the first transaction that I had completed with the new structure, and I have done many more with mostly the same investors. The key is to do better than the 10-year cash flow statement and pay the investors on time. Exceed expectations. So far, I have not missed an equity payment check or had one late. Who I am in this: If you trust me with your money and invest in a project, you will get what you expect when you expect it or before.

There may come a time where something happens that prevents this from unfolding as each deal is created. I am not going to put much energy into this, but if it does, I now have the credibility with my partners and lenders such that they would believe me and have confidence in my plan to rectify it. I have not had to go there, **and I say I will not have to go there**. My relationship with what I say is powerful, and I say this not as a hope or wish, but as a creation of a future I have in this self-storage business and with my partners.

The key to my confidence in the deals I structure is my relationship with the financial plan that is created through the Valuator analysis software. I trust the 10-year cash flow, and so far, with one exception (which we will cover in the Case Study), have exceeded what was created on it. The next chapter goes in depth into why and how you can trust it as well.

Chapter 12
The Valuator

"A successful person is one who can lay a firm foundation with
the bricks others have thrown at them."
~ David Brinkley

L
et's take a deep look into how to use the Valuator Self-Storage Financial Analysis software. The key to whatever success
I may have had has been how successfully I have been able to
determine the future cash flows of a facility. I cannot guarantee you
will be successful from using this tool, but your chances are greatly
increased if you put in the right information. What you get as the
10-year cash flow output will only be as good as the data you put in.

Unit Mix Page

As stated in Chapter 5, it all begins here. Input the sizes of the facility's unit mix, numbers of each sizes, and the current pricing of each
size. Sounds simple, but make sure it is correct.

This page will tell you a lot about the facility. Immediately I
look for the non–climate controlled 10' x 10' number and pricing.
According to the Self Storage Association, the average size of all the
units in the United States is 104 square feet. In most instances, the
10' x 10' is the most frequently asked-for size. I can tell a lot about
the financial health of a facility by looking at the price of a facility's
10' x 10' units.

It was a big deal when in some markets this unit went over the
$100 per month mark. REITS will be in a market that approaches or

exceeds this benchmark. Facilities that have this size below the $65 per month mark, for the most part, are hard to make work financially for us, and it tells me that the market or sub-market may be oversaturated.

I only have so many hours a day I can work and so many calories a day I want to expend turning a project around. It costs about the same to build a facility anywhere in the country (excluding the land cost). So why is there such a variance in pricing for a product that has a fairly constant construction cost? Local supply and demand.

Every facility I have looked at that had 10' x 10's priced at $55 per month or lower had an oversupply of self-storage in the feasibility report. It has gotten to the point that if I see that pricing, I have no further interest. You will soon figure out your benchmarks through experience and designing a business plan.

I also pay close attention to the gross potential per square foot income for each type of self-storage unit (i.e., climate controlled and non–climate controlled). Then pay close attention to the overall price per square foot for the entire project. Much below $8.50 per square foot gross income (income before expenses) makes it hard to work for us.

The smaller the unit size, the more per square foot income you will get. If you are looking at a facility that has an average unit size of more than 135 square feet, the price per square foot will in most cases be lower than a facility that has an average unit size closer to 100 square feet. Facilities that have larger customer bases of commercial customers tend to have larger average unit sizes. The average facility has about a 20% commercial customer mix. It is good to know this, especially if you are adding space. If you want to increase the per-square-foot income, one thing you could do is to have more units, but smaller. Ultimately, the market determines what your optimal unit mix is, but I try to guide the market a little. Usually, a feasibility report can tell you what the optimal unit mix should be based on the analysis of all the unit sizes and occupancy rates in the submarket of the facility you are looking at.

We like to see at least 22% of the units being climate controlled.

That is not to say we will not consider a facility that does not have that, but we like to see that. REITS like to see around 30% climate controlled. We like to copy REITS because they have the resources to test and explore what works and does not work in this business. If they are doing something, it is because it works. For example, if they sell tenant insurance, it is because they make money off it. (Public Storage made $39 million in 2013 selling tenant insurance). We sell it now every place we can. REITS use call centers. Why? Because they work. We use call centers now. Why? Because REITS do.

Again, this is our model. What is yours?

Finally, I look at our overall pricing against the competitors in that market. Is the facility I am looking at the highest? I like it when it is not. We will soon be the highest (because we will have the best). If I do not feel I will ever be the highest, or equal in pricing to the highest, I generally will pass on a facility. Being the lowest is another valid business model—just not ours. I want to be the facility that makes the most money in a market or I am not going to spend my time, energy, and money on the project. To be the most expensive in a market, we have to be the best facility.

I can now get most answers I need by looking at this sheet and knowing what the competition charges in that market.

Assumptions Page

The Acquisition Price

Unlike the unit mix page, which is just raw data, here one begins to create the future of that facility. It starts with the acquisition price. We have all heard that this is the most important item in a deal. In many ways, what you pay for a facility determines the success of a project. I do not argue that. I have overpaid for projects, and it takes a long time to compensate for overpaying.

Again, it all goes back to your business plan and/or business model. Obviously, I want to pay the least I can for a project, but I do not want cheap projects. In most cases, if a project is in trouble, or 50% full or less, for example, there is a reason for that. I cannot tell you how many facilities I have seen that should never have been built. No market research ever went into them. Someone just owned some land and decided to build themselves "mini-storage". (I hate that name; it is self-storage!) This is a professional, retail-oriented business. The days of industrial parks, backyards, and just a small one on extra land are over. If you have to compete with sophisticated operators, you should approach this business carefully. Know the supply and demand in the area where you are considering building or buying. Know where your facility stacks up in relation to the others. Know what you can generate in income from a facility. And finally, know what your return on investment parameters are. I have no problem paying any price necessary if I can get my return. I will pay more than asking price if I have to, as long as I can get my return. I do not have to get a "deal" to feel like I have made a good decision. As long as I can hit my targets, and the facility meets our business guidelines, I will buy it. I actually want the seller to feel like he/she is making a good deal. Then the seller will be very supportive of me and assist however necessary to get me to close.

The acquisition price is the number I change the most. If I put in all the data, and I cannot get the return I need, I will adjust this item until I do get the return. Nine cases out of 10, you will know if the deal stands a chance. If it does not, I rarely waste my time writing offers or LOIs.

The other closing cost and legal fees are there so you can get your total cash cost in. I know what I usually spend with a lawyer to have the entity created (a new LLC or S Corporation) that will actually own the project and the cost to have the operating agreement all the partners will sign. You may not have this cost if you are purchasing on your own. I usually have about $5,000 to $15,000 in lending costs, depending on the loan size.

Income Increase

I have found I can average over the hold of a project a minimum of a 3% average annual income growth. During the recession, there were years I did not raise prices. However, when I could, I raised 6% or 8% and still averaged a 3% per year average income increase.

I cannot tell you the number of facilities I see where the owner has not raised prices in two, three, or 10 years. They think they are doing fine, so they let it ride.

This is a business. My expenses are increasing. (I have never seen utility costs get cheaper, and my water bill has never gone down, just up). If I get a tax reduction, I have had to pay someone to get that reduction. My business practice is to raise prices yearly. Best practices call for a price increase unit size by unit size at certain occupancy benchmarks, then an overall price increase for the rest of the facility yearly. In other words, when 10' x 10's are over 90% occupied, raise the price. I often just have an across-the-board price increase in the summer. For the Valuator financial analysis, I will input a 3% per year price increase.

Many REITS now practice unit price management, such as airlines and hotels offer. In other words, the pricing can change daily depending on the demand for that unit's size and its availability. I have seen prices for a particular unit change monthly for existing customers in some of these facilities. We do not offer that pricing model yet and may never (never say never). Right now I am able to attract customers from facilities with that practice by having "stable" pricing. ("We just have yearly increases that are so small you will never notice.")

Expense Increase

I also assume a 2.5% inflation factor. If inflation starts to rise, use the accurate number. Then adjust the price increase to a higher percentage. I will always have a half a percent difference between price increase and inflation on my Valuator financial analysis. In practice, I try to have this be a full percent or more, but on the Valuator financial analysis it is just a half a percent. *This is what creates wealth over time in this business.* You will see on the 10-year cash flow statement the ROI (return on investment) increasing yearly. This is called compounding. Each year you are increasing the return percentage on the same amount of initial investment.

While the magic of compounding has led to the apocryphal

story of Albert Einstein supposedly calling it the eighth wonder of the world and/or man's greatest invention, compounding can also work against somebody if your expenses increase over your income year after year. For my business model, this is the art of it. I know I can create real equity by compounding the ROI each year. In fact, I know, almost to the year, when I will be able to refinance and get all the initial investment funds back and still have a new, refinanced loan at a 65% loan to value or less. I can create the value a number of ways, such as more square footage, lower operating expenses, better collection, etc. But a major component is my confidence in my ability to raise income over expenses each year. This is one of the main reasons I love this business so much. With what other commercial real estate asset can you do this year after year?

Stabilized Occupancy

I may be wrong, but in most markets I am in now, it appears as if the stabilized occupancy has gone up. I learned in my formative years from working with the REITS, and from all the feasibility reports I have funded and read, that for institutional-grade facilities (i.e., more than 50,000 square feet, etc.) stabilized occupancy should be around 85%. In other words, when a facility reaches its equilibrium, and one looks at the average occupancy in a 12-month period, it will average 85% physical occupancy.

I was told that for smaller facilities of less than 50,000 square feet, this number may be closer to 90%.

However, in recent years, most facilities I have seen are stabilizing or averaging more than 90%. For now, I am still using 85% as the stabilized occupancy in my financial analysis. As far as I know, most lenders are still using 85% as stabilized occupancy, so I do not want to work up a project only to have a lender say I did it wrong. It could be as simple as very little new square feet came online during the recession, so there is pent-up demand. It could be as fundamental as the fact that more people are now using self-storage (imagine what a 2% increase in the population using self-storage would mean to each facility).

For whatever the reason, I am still using 85%, even if the feasibility report indicated it is more than that figure. I feel safer using it, and if the project works at 85%, it will work at 90%.

Reversion CAP Rate

The value of commercial real estate is determined by what a ready, willing, and able buyer will pay for a particular income stream. The income stream is called the net operating income (NOI). To determine what a facility will be worth next year, two years from now, five years from now, and so on, one has to know two things: (1) the income stream and (2) the rate of return a buyer will use to value the project, generating the income stream. In other words, a capitalization rate (CAP rate). Reversion just means when you sell the project.

This program will determine the value of the facility each year by taking whatever reversion CAP rate you put in and dividing the NOI in a given year by it. The reversion CAP rate is used to determine the value of a project in future years.

How will you know what the market CAP rate will be in five or 10 years? You will not. However, you can have a good guess. What was it five years ago? I generally will look at what the current CAP rates are, and then increase them for the reversion CAP rate. The higher the CAP rate, the lower the value.

I have been amazed at how low interest rates for loans remain, and I am amazed at how low CAP rates have remained. I am not an economist, but there appears to be a correlation. If interest rates rise, I am guessing CAP rates will as well. So in my assumptions, I assume CAP rates are going to rise. This gives me a safe financial analysis and one I can usually outperform (or at least can so far).

If I am purchasing the facility on an 8% CAP rate, I will use a 9% reversion cap rate. Again, as a habit, I use a higher CAP rate to determine future values than the CAP rate I used to purchase the property.

Debt Service

I keep my finger on the pulse of what the commercial loan market is. If you are not sure, call your banker and ask. My experience is that most bank loans are on 20-year amortizations, require 25% to

35% down payment, and will have a three-, five-, or seven-year call. (See Chapter 5 for more detail on commercial loans).

Put in the details of the loan you anticipate for the project, and if you are going to be presenting this Valuator financial analysis to the banker, have your interest rate slightly lower than what you anticipate you can get (just a habit of mine).

One of the last assumptions is how much money you think you are going to spend the first year. This is for deferred maintenance to get it up to your standards (computers, signs, etc.) —all of the things that you will need to cause a switch of ownership and upgrade to your standards. Sometimes the figure is zero if the property is in great shape.

New Construction of Expansion

If the project requires an expansion, or if you are buying land and building a facility, click this tab and begin filling out. If you need an average cost for construction, there are a lot of resources out there, such as the *Self Storage Almanac* average construction cost. This can be a reference or a builder can be a reference.

One of the great benefits of this business is the low cost of the product. There are a number of high-quality manufacturers of self-storage buildings I highly recommend using. The days of a general contractor merely building using material he buys from his local suppliers are over. Even Butler Building systems has a relationship with one of these self-storage manufacturers, and if someone orders a Butler Building self-storage system, if is fabricated by one of the major suppliers of self-storage. These systems run from $5 to $12 per square foot depending on grade, style, interior systems or exterior systems, and if they are one-story or two-story and support bearing.

Many of the manufacturers will erect them for you, or you can hire your own erection crew. I highly recommend, if you hire a crew, to hire one that is certified to erect the system being purchased so you can get the warranties the manufacturing company offers. (Their warranties are among the big benefits of using these systems). There is a whole extra module if you are going to add new space or construct a new facility in the Valuator software program. I am not an expert here, and there are a lot of experts in the construction field. In fact, everyone I know that is an "expert" knows better than the next person what is the best way and pricing, and each "expert" always can see the flaws in the other experts' construction methods.

I am at the point where I know what expansions and new construction cost us, but I make a lot of mistakes here. I usually use a 10% contingency factor in each area (such as hard cost, soft cost, site work, etc.) and then a final contingency on the whole project. If I do that, all my misses are compensated for. Many readers will know much better than I do the construction cost.

This software has a line item construction budget that can be expanded on. These are just the lines I have used in the past, and we reserve the right to alter this as best practices change and evolve in this industry.

***

I fill out all of the areas of the analysis program initially using assumptions and data from my experience (if you are beginning, use industry averages), and then I replace my assumptions with the real numbers I get throughout the due diligence period. Once I have all the facts I am going to get, or all the bids for the construction, I then look at the 10-year cash flow page and see if it fits in my business plan. If it does I close. If it doesn't, I see what needs to happen so that it does and talk with the seller or the seller's agent. My posture is this: "I would like to purchase, but if not this one, then I will be buying the next one I can, so it is up to you, the seller. I really don't care which specific project I buy; I am executing a strategic business plan and I will fulfill the plan with or without your project." (I do not say it exactly like that).

One of the tendencies is to change the assumptions to generate the numbers you need to make the deal work. Attempt to avoid that habit. Do not reduce the expenses to get your numbers unless you are 100% sure you can achieve that reduction. I am here to tell you the years of problems that habit can create. I experienced that with the first deal that got me back into the business again, which you'll see in the Case Study. (It has an income assumption that caused me years of problems).

Use this analysis software to grow your business. If you are careful about what gets put in and you make sure of your accuracy, the 10-year cash flow page is an invaluable tool in creating wealth in this business.

10-Year Cash Flow Page

Usually the first place my eyes go is the first year's income. I look at it then take a quick glance at the seller's previous full-year's income to make sure there is not a large discrepancy. There should not be unless I am adding other profit centers like truck rental income, retail sales income, or tenant insurance income. If I am adding any new profit centers, I try to make the new income streams very conservative in my assumptions.

Next I look at year one's expenses and compare to the seller's. I should know, as I put in the assumptions, if I have more or less than the seller. I am usually higher because: (1) I pay more in salaries and (2) sellers rarely put in everything they spend. I do.

Next I glance at year one's net operating income (NOI) and see how different it is from what the seller has in his package. Whatever my year one NOI is divided by the sales price, that is my "going in" CAP rate. A lot of buyers make the "going in" CAP rate their primary benchmark for whether to buy or not. I do not. For self-storage, if that was my benchmark, there would be very few I purchase. It is not that I don't care, but I really care a lot more about other factors. For my plan, I am looking for two main items: (1) Can I create enough equity by the end of year five to refinance and pay all of the down payment back? and (2) Is there enough cash flow and extra refinance proceeds after paying back the down payment to give the investors 12% per year for the first five years? If the answer is yes to these, the deal works for me regardless of the "going in" CAP rate.

Decide your plan.

Your disposition CAP rate used in the assumptions will tell you the values at the bottom of each year in the "reversion sales price" line. I monitor that closely after I purchase a facility each year to make sure I am on track to complete our plan. In most cases, I am ahead. In other words, my NOI is higher than on the 10-year cash flow page and I know, if appraised today, what the real market CAP rate is. Hopefully, the market CAP rate is lower than what you put in the assumption page "reversion CAP rate." This is one of the main ways you can outperform your 10-year cash flow page.

It is easy to see the magic of compounding on this page. Look at how the ROI increases each year. Again what is happening is the income is rising faster than the expenses, increasing the return on the initial cash investment each year. In year one a project may only be spinning off 7% ROI, but I still may be able to pay the 12% per year because I know I will be compounding. By year five the same project may be at 18% and by year 10, 25%. All on the same number of units. This is why it is so important to raise rents each year. Even if you are at the top of the market (which we try to be), you raise them a dollar or two per unit. This is what creates the long-term wealth. If you are *not* going to do this, get in another business. I am amazed at the number of facilities I look at where it has been years since the last price increase, and then only new renters got the price increase. Just amazing. Tens and hundreds of thousands of dollars left on the table for someone else to get. Be the person who gets them, not the person who leaves them.

Case Study

"It was the best of times, it was the worst of times."
~ **Charles Dickens**

This case study looks at the acquisition of the project that got me back into the storage business in 2008. In many ways, this is the transaction I am the proudest of, and it is the one project that has not met the expectations of the 10-year cash flow statement—a worthy project to study.

Finding the Property

I found this property like I have found many others: An alarm went off in my computer that a new self-storage property had been listed in my target area. I see these at least weekly, sometimes more than one a day. At the time this property was beeped to me, I was discouraged. I had looked at a lot of self-storage facilities and had been unable to find one that I could purchase at the returns I needed to get back into the business. I was beginning to doubt my ability to be in this business again.

Five years earlier I was happily in the business, managing properties I had found and had put partnerships together on. We received an unsolicited offer from a regional REIT, and the way our LLC documents were set up, it took a simple majority vote to sell the properties. I was out of the business very fast. This time, I was determined not to have the same thing happen. I really wanted to be in for the long haul. I was just doubting if a person like me could really get in this business for the long haul.

There was nothing to indicate this was going to be the one I would purchase when that alarm went off. In fact, there were many reasons to think it was not. First of all, it was listed for more than $6 million dollars. It was only 86,450 square feet. That alone did not look promising. I almost passed right then and there, but I had promised myself I would look at every self-storage property that became available in our market. I called the real estate agent who had it listed.

I knew him. The agent, Charlie, said that the owner had called him trying to find some racking (that should have been a clue; most self-storage operators do not need racking) and Charlie talked him into listing the property to "test the waters".

The property was located on about 4.5 acres and was constructed in 2000 through 2001. It was cut block (a decorative block as opposed to concrete block or steel), and had shingle roofing and green roll-up doors. It is the only shingle roof facility I currently own. They are very expensive to replace. I did get the shingle roofs on all the buildings replaced from insurance proceeds after a wind storm a few years ago, a move that saved me more than $100,000, but now the property insurance premiums' for that property are very high. Steel roofs don't look as nice, but they are much more economical.

It turns out that this property was owned by the father and son team who built it. The son had run into some money selling a business, and the father was a builder. The son told the father he could bankroll him in constructing their first self-storage project if he could be a partner. They started constructing.

Like many properties I have seen built by builders, this one is over-built—not as bad as many, but over-built in terms of cost and materials. One of the reasons I like dealing with self-storage manufacturing companies is that the cost is the most economical. At the stage this project was in when I was considering it, I was not going to buy the quality or cost of construction, but rather the income flow. However, the higher cost of construction still puts a higher value in the mind of the seller if he is the one who built it.

As I showed up for the tour, something went off in my head that I would own this one. I cannot say what it was, but I have felt it before.

It is like an intuition. I knew as I walked up to the door that it was a trip I would make many times.

I received the tour from the agent and the owner. It was a nice-looking property. They were around 85% occupied, and it had a "record storage" component to it. (I should have run right there). I was unfamiliar with record storage, but the owner told me it was great and that if I didn't like it, he could break it off because he would love to keep it.

In hindsight, I should have done that. Hindsight is always more clear. He created that business from nothing and was very proud of it. It was not my core competency, and I have learned over and over that when I get away from my core competencies, life gets hard.

It appeared as if his self-storage had been absorbed to stabilization at about 5% of the square footage per month, which tells me the market liked it and the pricing was in line. I liked all of that. A quick run with my calculator, however, indicated about $4.6 to $5.0 million in value at the time, depending on the cap rate. The owner indicated he knew that, but the difference was the record storage.

He said if I did my research, I would see that record storage grew at an average rate of 18% per year (his project had increased higher than that over the past two years) and that it was very difficult to lose customers because it cost a lot for them to leave and go to a competitor (perm out fees), all of which turned out to be true. He also loved the record storage business because it took square foot income (self-storage rent) and turned it into cubic foot income. (Record storage is charged by the cubic foot of storage and boxes can be stacked to the ceiling). I was very intrigued. How hard could it be? So I went to work analyzing the project.

Analysis

I used my Valuator program and input the storage information. Since there was nothing in the program for a record storage component, I just created another line item in the income area for it. I took his last 12 months' income, raised it by 18%, then used that figure as my first

12 months' income, and then added an 18% growth factor per year to it to get future cash flows.

That may seem silly to you now, sitting there reading this, but to me at the time, I saw it as a way to get back in the business. I sure wish I had not done that, but I did. I was bullish off the 2005 through 2007 times where real estate was increasing in value very fast. I previewed this project in the summer of 2007. Things were going great. I had his last few years as backup, and all information I read at the time indicated that record storage companies usually grow their storage by 15% to 20% per year. It did not seem too farfetched at the time, and at the time it wasn't.

You will see from the first year on the 10-year Financial analysis on page 117, I had storage income and a line item called late fees. I still track my late fees, but I no longer include them in the Valuator financial analysis. I do this for a number of reasons, but primarily because on this deal I missed by almost this exact amount in the first-year storage income, so to be safe, I have taken them out. Also, partners were focused on this line item, and I would rather have them focused on total income and not get bogged down on late-fee philosophies.

You will also notice an income of $256,000 for record storage. That was what the current owner said he was going to get over the next 12 months. Then I raised it 18% each year after. A miss. However, the self-storage income numbers I used then have tracked almost exactly as predicted.

I wrote a letter of intent and then a contract, and put the property under contract for $6.25 million, what I thought was a good value at more than a 12% CAP. I had two months to remove all my contingencies.

Storage Plus

PROJECTED CASH FLOWS

END OF YEAR	1	2	3	4	5	6	7	8	9	10
REVENUES										
Rent Revenues										
GPI	585,756	603,329	621,429	640,071	659,274	679,052	699,423	720,406	742,018	764,279
Net Rental Rev.	477,775	492,109	506,872	522,078	537,740	553,873	570,489	587,603	605,231	623,388
Other Revenues										
Net Taxable Sales	3,000	3,090	3,183	3,278	3,377	3,478	3,582	3,690	3,800	3,914
Other Admin Revenues	4,907	5,054	5,206	5,362	5,523	5,689	5,859	6,035	6,216	6,403
Records Storage	256,026	302,111	356,491	420,659	496,378	585,726	691,157	815,565	962,366	1,136,592
Late Fees	31,591	32,538	33,514	34,520	35,555	36,622	37,721	38,852	40,018	41,219
Truck Rental Commissions	5,432	5,595	5,763	5,936	6,114	6,297	6,486	6,681	6,881	7,088
Total Other Revenues	300,956	348,389	404,157	469,755	546,947	637,812	744,005	870,823	1,019,282	1,194,216
TOTAL REVENUES	778,731	840,497	911,029	991,833	1,084,687	1,191,684	1,315,294	1,458,426	1,624,514	1,817,604
OPERATING EXPENSES										
Bank Service Charges	5,763.71	5,937	6,115	6,298	6,487	6,682	6,882	7,089	7,301	7,520
Contract Labor	932.86	961	990	1,019	1,050	1,081	1,114	1,147	1,182	1,217
Insurance	10,368.00	10,679	10,999	11,329	11,669	12,019	12,380	12,751	13,134	13,528
Workers Comp Insurance	1,375.98	1,417	1,460	1,504	1,549	1,595	1,643	1,692	1,743	1,795
Lawn Care	1,156.44	1,191	1,227	1,264	1,302	1,341	1,381	1,422	1,465	1,509
Marketing	36,521.79	37,617	38,746	39,908	41,106	42,339	43,609	44,917	46,265	47,653
Office Supplies	6,166.33	6,351	6,542	6,738	6,940	7,148	7,363	7,584	7,811	8,046
Payroll	64,478.15	66,412	68,405	70,457	72,571	74,748	76,990	79,300	81,679	84,129
Postage	2,032.20	2,093	2,156	2,221	2,287	2,356	2,427	2,499	2,574	2,652
Professional Fees	2,574.15	2,651	2,731	2,813	2,897	2,984	3,074	3,166	3,261	3,359
Referral Fee	509.92	525	541	557	574	591	609	627	646	665
Repairs	1,561.46	1,608	1,657	1,706	1,757	1,810	1,864	1,920	1,978	2,037
Taxes	68,250.00	70,298	72,406	74,579	76,816	79,120	81,494	83,939	86,457	89,051
Utilities	21,024.20	21,655	22,305	22,974	23,663	24,373	25,104	25,857	26,633	27,432
Total Storage Expenses:	222,715.19	229,396.65	236,278.55	243,366.90	250,667.91	258,187.95	265,933.58	273,911.59	282,128.94	290,592.81
Record Storage Expense										
Delivery	7,866.02	8,102	8,345	8,595	8,853	9,119	9,392	9,674	9,964	10,263
Destruction Expense	73.54	76	78	80	83	85	88	90	93	96
Indexing Labor	6,453.00	6,647	6,846	7,051	7,263	7,481	7,705	7,936	8,174	8,420
Record Storage Comm	180.69	186	192	197	203	209	216	222	229	236
Record Storage Boxes	2,432.13	2,505	2,580	2,658	2,737	2,820	2,904	2,991	3,081	3,173
Truck	186.11	192	197	203	209	216	222	229	236	243
Van Expense	2,000.00	2,060	2,122	2,185	2,251	2,319	2,388	2,460	2,534	2,610
Van Gas	1,096.25	1,119	1,152	1,187	1,223	1,259	1,297	1,336	1,376	1,417
Total Record Storage Expense:	20,277.75	20,886.09	21,512.67	22,158.05	22,822.79	23,507.48	24,212.70	24,939.08	25,687.25	26,457.87

Management Fee 2.40%	18,689.55	20,171.93	21,864.69	23,804.00	26,032.49	28,600.43	31,567.05	35,002.23	38,988.33	43,622.50
TOTAL OPERATING EXPENSE	261,682.50	270,454.67	279,655.91	289,328.95	299,523.19	310,295.85	321,713.34	333,852.90	346,804.52	360,673.18
NET OPERATING INCOME	517,049	570,043	631,373	702,504	785,164	881,389	993,581	1,124,573	1,277,709	1,455,931
DEBT SERVICE										
Debt Service Perm. 1	$360,853	$360,853	$360,853	$360,853	$360,853	$360,853	$360,853	$360,853	$360,853	$360,853
Mez. Loan	$135,019	$135,019	$135,019	$135,019	$135,019	$135,019	$135,019	$0	$0	$0
TOTAL DEBT SERVICE	$495,872	$495,872	$495,872	$495,872	$495,872	$495,872	$495,872	$360,853	$360,853	$360,853
Reserve Fund	$ 12,886	$ 12,886	$ 12,886	$ 12,886	$ 12,886	$ 12,886	$ 12,886	$ 12,886	$ 12,886	12,886
NET CASH FLOW										
Commerce	21,177	61,285	122,615	193,746	276,406	372,631	484,823	750,834	903,970	1,083,192
Q-II Plus	16,942	49,028	98,092	154,997	221,125	298,105	387,858	600,667	723,176	866,553
	4,235	12,257	24,523	38,749	55,281	74,526	96,965	150,167	180,794	216,638
% ROC	1.79%	5.17%	10.35%	16.36%	23.34%	31.46%	40.93%	63.39%	76.32%	91.46%
REVERSION SALES PRICE		6,333,807	7,015,255	7,805,604	8,724,045	9,793,207	11,039,784	12,495,259	14,196,769	16,188,121
COST OF SALE (5%)		316,690	350,763	390,280	436,202	489,660	551,989	624,763	709,838	809,406
ASSET MGMT. FEE (1%)		63,338	70,153	78,056	87,240	97,932	110,398	124,953	141,968	161,881
1st LOAN BALANCE	4,549,460	4,458,654	4,382,256	4,259,923	4,151,289	4,035,966	3,913,543	3,783,581	3,645,618	3,499,160
MEX LOAN BALANCE	569,812	466,108	356,020	239,153	115,090	(16,611)	(156,422)	(304,841)	(462,398)	(629,657)
PROCEEDS AVAILABLE	-	1,029,016	1,876,063	2,836,192	3,934,222	5,186,260	6,620,276	8,266,803	10,161,743	12,347,331
Commerce		950,000	1,500,851	2,270,553	3,147,378	4,149,008	5,296,221	6,613,442	8,129,394	9,877,865
Q-II, Plus		79,016	375,213	567,638	786,844	1,037,252	1,324,055	1,653,361	2,032,349	2,469,466
NET C-F + S/R + REV.		1,090,301	1,998,678	3,031,938	4,210,629	5,558,890	7,105,099	9,017,637	11,065,713	13,430,523

The Deal

I next went out to put a deal together. In my last incarnation as a storage company, I had hired a woman as an area manager, overseeing the facility managers out of state. She was good. She had married into a family with some wealth, and they owned a self-storage facility she was helping with. I went to her husband's family and presented the deal. There were three brothers and a father. Some were more excited than others, but the father seemed to like the project and see the potential of the deal. I got the thumbs-up that they were going to most likely be in.

I next went and met with a commercial mortgage broker. I indicated I was looking for non-recourse financing, which was plentiful in the summer of 2007. I showed the deal I had under contract and he indicated he did not see an issue. Things were rolling.

I next met with an attorney and asked him to draw up the LLC documents as I discussed with the family. I actually had some time to spare. Inspections were happening; all was well with the world.

That is how it usually happens; it is quiet before the storm.

The inspections came back with no real issues. Two weeks before the contingencies were to be removed, I received a call from the family saying there was a lot of internal squabbling, and they were not going to invest in the deal. It was obvious I had misread them. I only had two weeks left to find a million dollars, the down payment needed for the deal.

I made a couple of calls but was really dejected. I saw no hope, but I was not going to give in. I had 10 days left.

On a Thursday morning, I went to a Real Estate Exchangors marketing session. (This is a forum of commercial real estate agents and owners of commercial real estate who get together and market income-producing real estate using creative methods, such as exchanging). Around 10:00 a.m., I saw a vacant industrial building with a value of $1.25 million, no loans on it, being presented by an agent. When someone asked that agent who the owner was, the agent said the name of a person I recognized. When I first went into commercial real estate, that person was a "for sale by owner"

(FSBO), and I listed and sold a commercial building he owned. I raised my hand and said, "I am a taker for the building, but we have to meet today."

The agent and I went straight over to the owner's office and I showed him the storage project projections. I said I would take his industrial building and I would give him a 70% ownership in this project for his equity in the industrial building. He must have sensed my desperation because he said he would consider if it was 80%. I agreed. Within four hours of getting up that Thursday morning, I had the deal back.

That owner was a retired CPA. He had created wealth by exchanging his equity, deferring the capital gains, and putting all his equity to work, getting in larger and larger deals every time. By taking his building, I knew I could "crank," or refinance the building and put an 80% loan on the building, thus raising my needed million dollars for the down payment. He would be able to complete a 1031 tax deferred exchange, and put his equity into this larger deal and make even more money. He was retired, so the non-recourse financing was particularly appealing to him, and I knew it would be.

What I saw as the risk at the time was the empty building, but I had a plan for it. The core group at that time was a father and son investment team and me. The father and son were clients I had sold a lot of investment real estate to. They had some money to invest in more real estate, and I asked them if they would like to be partners on a self-storage project. As I was negotiating this deal, I knew they had some money they would invest for their ownership percentage. We were the 20% owners of the deal being negotiated, and the owner of the industrial building was the 80%. Since I had enough equity from the cranked building, the father and son team's money that was to be put in the deal was instead going to service the debt on the vacant building until we found a tenant. We were going to own less of the storage facility than we initially planned, but we also owned a $1.2 million industrial building together.

All was right with the world. I just needed a few more extra weeks to get the financing on the industrial building in place. I went to the seller of the storage facility and indicated I could remove most of the contingencies but needed a few weeks extra. I was surprised how hard he was to deal with at that point. He was at first a "no," wondering what was going on and not believing what I was telling him. Then finally, after lawyers, letters, and calls, I got a few extra weeks with the good-faith deposit becoming non-refundable. That was way harder than it had to be, but it worked.

After getting the financing for the industrial building in place, I removed the contingencies, we closed on the industrial building, and the funds went into an "accommodators" account (like an escrow account for 1031 funds so our 80% partner didn't touch the proceeds, thus invalidating the 1031 exchange) and we were ready to close on the storage facility.

Then the real storm hit. I don't know if you remember the meltdown toward the end of 2007 and beginning of 2008, but I do. It was as if this deal was at the center of it all. On a Tuesday, I got a call from the mortgage broker who had placed the non-recourse conduit loan we were going to use on the storage facility. We were trying to schedule the closing of the storage facility, and he was being a little evasive. Finally that morning he called and said we had "lost" part of our funding. That was a term I had never heard. Well, apparently he had not either, until that day. Apparently, the financing we had arranged was to be placed into packages of loans that were "securitized" (sold) on Wall Street. That is where the lender's money was going to come from to fund our loan. Wall Street was melting, and there was no market for these loans. By the end of the week, all this type of financing had stopped. It would be close to 2010 before it would start up again.

So there we were: one million dollars of the 80% partner's money in an account ready to close, me and the father and son team the proud owners of a vacant (operable word here) industrial building, no financing for the storage in place, and two weeks to close. I remembered how much fun the seller was before; I knew we were going to have a ball now.

I had never seen anything like this happen before, and we were all in uncharted territory. There was no resource to help us. I couldn't Google what to do, because this had never happened before. It is still amazing to me how in less than a week things so totally melted down. I went with my hat in my hand to the 80% partner and told him, "I really need some help now. Anything—any coaching you could give me—I would appreciate."

The Rest of the Story

I will always appreciate how cool a head my 80% partner had during that time. I have learned a lot from him, but probably more during those weeks and months than from any mentor in my career. His coaching was simple ("keep your eye on the ball"), but who he was *being* gave me hope. He just said, "Take one step at a time and do what is necessary not to lose my money and close the deal."

There was only one item that I needed: an extension from the storage owner. I needed a little more time to get a new loan in place. My 80% partner said that if I could get the extension, he would get the financing.

The seller was as much fun as I anticipated. The short version is this: The million dollars had to become non-refundable; if we did not close in 60 days, he would get it. The 80% owner was so certain he could get the financing through his bank, he was willing to risk it.

He got in essence two loans: one for the self-storage and one for the record storage that was on paper—very close to the original financing I had in place, but with one major difference: Everyone had to guarantee the loan. We thought this financing was going to take a few weeks to get. It turned out to be much longer. The banks were very scared at that time. A lot happened between our Wall Street meltdown and the closing that took place on February 28, 2008 (seven months after I first saw the property). Lehman Brother collapsed, AIG was bailed out, and—well, you know the story. Suffice it to say, banks were jumpy.

Finally, we had been "approved" and I was attempting to schedule the closing of the storage facility. The bank had to have the appraisals looked at again, the facility's year-end numbers had to be looked at again as well, and on and on. The closing got moved back. January's numbers were now required. February 28 was the last day before the 80% owner's money would go hard (i.e., the seller of the storage facility would get the money in escrow and the deal would be off). The seller of the storage facility didn't care if it closed. In fact, he was better off if it didn't.

On the morning of the closing, on the last day before the money was going hard, I received a call from the 80% partner. He said that the bank had decided to change the amortization on the second loan (the one for the record storage business portion of the deal) from 20 years to six years because "it wasn't real estate; it was a business." On the day of the closing! This sent my loan payment up more than $10,000 per month. If we did not close, the 80% partner lost his million dollars. We had to close and the bank knew it.

On February 28, 2008, I was back in the self-storage business. It was not like I pictured, but I was in it again.

Operations

Since this is a book about acquiring self-storage, I will not spend a lot of time going over what happened after we purchased the facility. Suffice it to say it was a challenging first few years. We lost about 5% to 6% occupancy (overall not bad) of storage customers. We had to spend a lot of energy on collections. Self-storage really showed its value during the recession. It is not recession-proof, but it is certainly recession-resistant.

The record storage business was another story. This industry is a business-to-business industry. It lost 20% or so of business and was very slow to recover. It is also an industry in change, with less paper coming in for storage. I will just say we did not grow at the 18% I projected.

The Takeaways

I chose this as the case study because there was a lot done right, and a lot done wrong. It is the only deal I have purchased to date that did not exceed the projections on the 10-year cash flow sheet. As a business owner, we learn more from our mistakes than our successes, so I could not have picked a better case study.

I remember the day of the closing saying to myself, "No matter what happens, we got this deal to close. No one can ever take that away." I learned just how creative I can be to make a deal happen. "The key to success is often how well you can implement Plan B." I think I made that up after this deal. There is always a way to make a deal happen if you want to. We are only limited by our own thinking. Once I set my mind on making this deal, the opportunities were everywhere. The key was I set my mind on getting it, and then was aware and present. When a human being sets a powerful intention, the universe will then bend itself to fulfill that intention. Our job is to set the intention, then act and take what is given us.

My intention now is a $60 million storage portfolio. Do you want to take bets that I don't make it?

What *real intention* have you created that you focus on daily? Organize your life for its fulfillment.

However, I also did a lot of things wrong here that I have not repeated since. The first and foremost lesson I learned was when I get away from my core competencies, I create the space for failure. The record storage business is a great business—just not for me. I liked the idea of it, but not the business itself. It is different from storage, and I was not honest with myself that I would take the time to learn it or to grow it.

I also should have valued the record storage component like a separate business, not as self-storage. In self-storage one places a value on the income stream by using a CAP rate. In most business the value is some multiples of gross or net income with another value for furniture, fixtures, equipment, customers, and good will. I used a CAP rate on the record-storage income stream to value it, not a more reliable business valuation model.

However, we hung in there, put in cash when necessary, and paid the fast-amortizing loan down. We now have some real equity. I have never put as high a percentage of debt on another project since then, either. Time will make up for any mistakes made during acquisition. We are now in a good loan to value position, and I am paying a return to the 80% partner as projected. It just took six years to get there. (I must say here this partner was great and very understanding. I have learned a lot by being his partner, and I think the real essence of someone shows during hard times. This man was very patient and understanding with me. He was disappointed, but not accusatory. He always kept his "eye on the ball" and did not make the people in the transaction wrong and bad).

I now never go over 70% loan to value, and in most of my deals since then, I put a 65% LTV in place. Leverage is great. It can make a deal perform very well, but it can also bite you. I got bit and learned my lesson. If I can't make the deal work at 65% or 70% LTV, I let someone else make that deal work for them.

The last takeaway that may affect you if you use the Valuator financial analysis software program is that I took the late fees out of the Valuator as an income line item. If you make more income than projected from the late fees, great. But they are not the primary income stream or part of a business model, and I decided to focus on people paying their rent on time, not being late at my profit. Since I have done that, I have had great luck in my acquisitions. (I am never superstitious. Well, almost never.)

The last, last thing I would say here concerning this deal was that, since my investing partner was not making any money during the first five years of the deal (we were paying the bank, not him, due to the short-term loan given on the day of closing), I took no management fee. If you put the deals together and they do not pay out, let your investors start getting money first before you take any. You may not hit every deal as projected, but they can still refer you. In the final analysis, your reputation and how you do business are the only real things you take into your meetings. I have made a lot of mistakes over my career, but you only have to do a few things right to have a successful career and create real wealth. Your ability to be transparent, be honest, and do business like you would want others to do it with you are the only things that can ensure the marathon run. Especially, when this business is over the short sprint of a single deal. Be a long-distance entrepreneur.

10-Year Financial Analysis

Storage Plus

SUMMARY FINANCIAL INFORMATION AND ASSUMPTIONS

Project Location

Year Project Starts   2008

REVENUES		Year 1		Year 2		Year 3		Year 4		Year 5
REVENUES	$	778,731	$	840,497	$	911,029	$	991,833	$1,084,687
OP. EXPENSES	$	261,682	$	270,455	$	279,656	$	289,329	$	299,523
NET OP. INCOME	$	517,049	$	570,043	$	631,373	$	702,504	$	785,164
DEBT SERVICE	$	495,872	$	495,872	$	495,872	$	495,872	$	495,872
NET CASH FLOW	$	21,177	$	61,285	$	122,615	$	193,746	$	276,406
CASH-ON-CASH RETURN		2.24%		6.47%		12.94%		20.45%		29.17%

	Gross S.F.	Per Gross S.F.	Rentable S.F.	Per Rentable S.F.	Gross $
PROJECT COST					
Acquisition Cost					
Facility Cost	85,908	$ 72.75	77,908	$ 80.22	$6,250,000
Closing Cost					$ 2,000
Market Study		$ 0.06		$ 0.06	$ 5,000
Environmental Study		$ 0.02		$ 0.03	$ 2,000
Lending Fees		$ -		$ -	$ -
Total Acq. Cost	85,908	$ 72.86	77,908	$ 80.34	$6,259,000
TOTAL PROJECT COST	**85,908**	**$ 72.86**	**77,908**	**$ 80.34**	**$6,259,000**

	Gross S.F.	Per Gross S.F.	Rentable S.F.	Per Rentable S.F.	Gross $
POTENTIAL GROSS INCOME					
(Based upon Total S.F.)					
Existing Facility	85,908	$ 6.82	67,908	$ 8.63	$ 585,756

ANNUAL DEBT SERVICE (Permanent)	$360,853
EFFICIENCY (Rentable s.f./Gross s.f.) Existing Facility	79.05%
ANNUAL SS REV. GROWTH	3.00%
ANNUAL RS REV. GROWTH	18.00%
ANNUAL EXPENSE GROWTH	2.50%

YEAR 1 CAPITAL IMPROVEMENTS	$0	
RESERVE FUND	$0.15	Per square Foot
PERFERRED CS TO COMMERCE	8%	
REVERSION CAP RATE	9.00%	

PERMANENT FINANCING

Debt	$	4,635,000
LTV Ratio		74%
Rate		5.99%
Amortization		25

SECOND MORTGAGE

Debt	$	667,500
LTV Ratio		11%
Rate		5.99%
Amortization		6
Commerce Properties, LLC		80%
Q-II Plus, LLC		20%
		100%

Ccommerce Properties

Start Up Capital	$	947,500
	$	-
TOTAL	$	947,500

Storage Plus

PROJECTED DEBT SERVICE

ACTUAL COST IN PROJECT

Acquisition Cost	$6,250,000
TOTAL COST IN PROJECT	$ 6,250,000
YEAR 1 CAPITAL IMPROVEMENTS	$ -
BASIS IN IMPROVEMENTS	$ 6,250,000
	$ 947,500
EQUITY IN PROJECT*	$ 1,615,000

PERMANENT FINANCING

Loan Amount	LTV Ratio	Term in Months	Interest Rate	Monthly Payment	Ann. Debt Service
$ 4,635,000	74%	300	5.99%	$30,071	**$360,853**

SECOND MORTGAGE

Loan Amount	LTV Ratio	Term in Months	Interest Rate	Monthly Payment	Ann. Debt Service
$ 667,500	11%	72	5.99%	$11,252	**$135,018.60**

$41,323

Storage Plus

UNIT MIX - EXISTING

	Unit Size	Unit S.F.	#Units	Total S.F.	% of Total S.F.	Monthly Unit Price	Annual Rent/S.F.	Monthly GPI	Annual GPI
NCC	5 x 5	25	22	550	0.81%	$ 39.00	$ 18.72	$ 858	$ 10,296
	6 x 16	96	1	96	0.14%	$ 73.00	$ 9.13	$ 73	$ 876
	5 x 12	60	2	120	0.18%	$ 60.00	$ 12.00	$ 120	$ 1,440
	5 x 10	50	42	2,100	3.09%	$ 55.00	$ 13.20	$ 2,310	$ 27,720
	6 x 10	60	3	180	0.27%	$ 60.00	$ 12.00	$ 180	$ 2,160
	8 x 10	80	3	240	0.35%	$ 75.00	$ 11.25	$ 225	$ 2,700
	6 x 13	78	3	234	0.34%	$ 75.00	$ 11.54	$ 225	$ 2,700
	5 x 15	75	5	375	0.55%	$ 75.00	$ 12.00	$ 375	$ 4,500
	8 x 12	96	3	288	0.42%	$ 80.00	$ 10.00	$ 240	$ 2,880
	10 x 10	100	90	9,000	13.25%	$ 84.00	$ 10.08	$ 7,560	$ 90,720
	10 x 12	120	3	360	0.53%	$ 94.00	$ 9.40	$ 282	$ 3,384
	10 x 15	150	44	6,600	9.72%	$ 104.00	$ 8.32	$ 4,576	$ 54,912
	10 x 18	180	2	360	0.53%	$ 115.00	$ 7.67	$ 230	$ 2,760
	10 x 20	200	54	10,800	15.90%	$ 120.00	$ 7.20	$ 6,480	$ 77,760
	10 x 26	260	22	5,720	6.66%	$ 139.00	$ 6.42	$ 3,058	$ 36,696
	10 x 30	300	32	9,600	14.14%	$ 170.00	$ 6.80	$ 5,440	$ 65,280
	20 x 26	520	1	520	0.77%	$ 275.00	$ 6.35	$ 275	$ 3,300
	10 x 40	400	16	6,400	9.42%	$ 209.00	$ 6.27	$ 3,344	$ 40,128
	30 x 30	900	1	900	1.33%	$ 520.00	$ 6.93	$ 520	$ 6,240
	20 x 30	600	2	1,200	1.77%	$ 350.00	$ 7.00	$ 700	$ 8,400
	40 x 30	1200	2	2,400	3.53%	$ 690.00	$ 6.90	$ 1,380	$ 16,560
	17 x 15	255	1	255	0.38%	$ 135.00	$ 6.35	$ 135	$ 1,620
	17 x 20	340	2	680	1.00%	$ 175.00	$ 6.18	$ 350	$ 4,200

Sub-total NCC			356	58,978	85.08%	$ 7.92	$ 38,936	$ 467,232
5 x 5	25	3	75	0.11%	$ 52.00	$ 24.96	$ 156	$ 1,872
5 x 10	50	11	550	0.81%	$ 75.00	$ 18.00	$ 825	$ 9,900
6 x 10	60	1	60	0.09%	$ 83.00	$ 16.60	$ 83	$ 996
5 x 15	75	3	225	0.33%	$ 87.00	$ 13.92	$ 261	$ 3,132
10 x 10	100	27	2,700	3.98%	$ 115.00	$ 13.80	$ 3,105	$ 37,260
10 x 13	130	2	260	0.38%	$ 135.00	$ 12.46	$ 270	$ 3,240
10 x 20	200	12	2,400	3.53%	$ 199.00	$ 11.94	$ 2,388	$ 28,656
10 x 15	150	6	900	1.33%	$ 149.00	$ 11.92	$ 894	$ 10,728
13 x 20	260	1	260	0.38%	$ 270.00	$ 12.46	$ 270	$ 3,240
10 x 30	300	5	1,500	2.21%	$ 325.00	$ 13.00	$ 1,625	$ 19,500
17 x 20	340	0	0	0.00%	$ 175.00	$ 6.18	$ -	$ -
Sub-total CC		71	8,930	13.15%		$ 13.27	$ 9,877	$ 118,524
Total		427	67,908	98.24%		$ 8.63	$ 48,813	$ 585,756

Average S.F. @ Unit	159.04
Gross S.F.	85,908
Efficiency	79.05%
Net Rentable S.F.	67,908

Storage Plus

PROJECTED CASH FLOWS

ANNUAL YEAR 1 THRU 10

END OF YEAR	1	2	3	4	5	6	7	8	9	10
REVENUES										
Rent Revenues										
GPI	585,756	603,329	621,429	640,071	659,274	679,052	699,423	720,406	742,018	764,279
Net Rental Rev.	477,775	492,109	506,872	522,078	537,740	553,873	570,489	587,603	605,231	623,388
Other Revenues										
Net Taxable Sales	3,000	3,090	3,183	3,278	3,377	3,476	3,582	3,690	3,800	3,914
Other Admin Revenues	4,907	5,054	5,206	5,362	5,523	5,689	5,869	6,035	6,216	6,403
Records Storage	256,026	302,111	356,491	420,659	496,378	585,726	691,157	815,565	962,366	1,135,592
Late Fees	31,591	32,538	33,514	34,520	35,555	36,622	37,721	38,852	40,018	41,219
Truck Rental Commissions	5,432	5,595	5,763	5,936	6,114	6,297	6,496	6,681	6,881	7,088
Total Other Revenues	300,956	348,389	404,157	469,766	546,947	637,812	744,805	870,823	1,019,282	1,194,216
TOTAL REVENUES	778,731	840,497	911,029	991,833	1,084,687	1,191,684	1,315,294	1,458,426	1,624,514	1,817,604
OPERATING EXPENSES										
Bank Service Charges	5,763.71	5,937	6,115	6,298	6,487	6,682	6,882	7,089	7,301	7,520
Contract Labor	932.86	961	990	1,019	1,050	1,081	1,114	1,147	1,182	1,217
Insurance	10,368.00	10,679	10,999	11,329	11,669	12,019	12,380	12,751	13,134	13,528
Workers Comp Insurance	1,375.98	1,417	1,460	1,504	1,549	1,595	1,643	1,692	1,743	1,795
Lawn Care	1,156.44	1,191	1,227	1,264	1,302	1,341	1,381	1,422	1,465	1,509
Marketing	36,521.79	37,617	38,746	39,908	41,106	42,339	43,609	44,917	46,265	47,653
Office Supplies	6,166.33	6,351	6,542	6,738	6,940	7,148	7,363	7,584	7,811	8,046
Payroll	64,478.15	66,412	68,405	70,457	72,571	74,748	76,990	79,300	81,679	84,129
Postage	2,032.20	2,093	2,156	2,221	2,287	2,356	2,427	2,499	2,574	2,652
Professional Fees	2,574.15	2,651	2,731	2,813	2,897	2,984	3,074	3,166	3,261	3,359
Referral Fee	509.92	525	541	557	574	591	609	627	646	665
Repairs	1,561.46	1,608	1,657	1,706	1,757	1,810	1,864	1,920	1,978	2,037
Taxes	68,250.00	70,298	72,406	74,579	76,816	79,120	81,494	83,939	86,457	89,051
Utilities	21,024.20	21,655	22,305	22,974	23,663	24,373	25,104	25,857	26,633	27,432
Total Storage Expenses:	222,715.19	229,396.65	236,278.55	243,366.90	250,667.91	258,187.95	265,933.58	273,911.59	282,128.94	290,592.81
Record Storage Expense										
Delivery	7,866.02	8,102	8,345	8,595	8,853	9,119	9,392	9,674	9,964	10,263
Destruction Expense	73.54	76	78	80	83	85	88	88	93	96
Indexing Labor	6,453.00	6,647	6,846	7,051	7,263	7,481	7,705	7,936	8,174	8,420
Record Storage Comm	180.69	186	192	197	203	209	216	222	229	236
Record Storage Boxes	2,432.13	2,505	2,580	2,658	2,737	2,820	2,904	2,991	3,081	3,173
Truck	186.11	192	197	203	209	216	222	229	236	243
Van Expense	2,000.00	2,060	2,122	2,185	2,251	2,319	2,388	2,460	2,534	2,610
Van Gas	1,086.25	1,119	1,152	1,187	1,223	1,259	1,297	1,336	1,376	1,417
Total Record Storage Expense:	20,277.75	20,886.09	21,512.67	22,158.05	22,822.79	23,507.48	24,212.70	24,939.08	25,687.25	26,457.87

	%	1	2	3	4	5	6	7	8	9	10
		18,689.55	20,171.93	21,864.69	23,604.00	26,032.49	28,600.43	31,567.05	35,002.23	38,988.33	43,622.50
Management Fee	2.40%										
TOTAL OPERATING EXPENSE		261,682.50	270,464.67	279,655.91	289,328.95	299,523.19	310,295.85	321,713.34	333,852.90	346,804.52	360,673.18
NET OPERATING INCOME		517,049	570,043	631,373	702,504	785,164	881,389	993,581	1,124,573	1,277,709	1,456,931
DEBT SERVICE											
Debt Service Perm. 1		$360,853	$360,853	$360,853	$360,853	$360,853	$360,853	$360,853	$360,853	$360,853	$360,853
Mez. Loan		$135,019	$135,019	$135,019	$135,019	$135,019	$135,019	$135,019	$0	$0	$0
TOTAL DEBT SERVICE		$495,872	$495,872	$495,872	$495,872	$495,872	$495,872	$495,872	$360,853	$360,853	$360,853
Reserve Fund		$ 12,886	$ 12,886	$ 12,886	$ 12,886	$ 12,886	$ 12,886	$ 12,886	$ 12,886	$ 12,886	$ 12,886
NET CASH FLOW		21,177	61,285	122,615	193,746	276,406	372,631	484,823	750,834	903,970	1,083,192
Commerce		16,942	49,028	98,092	154,997	221,125	298,105	387,858	600,667	723,176	866,553
Q-II Plus		4,235	12,257	24,523	38,749	55,281	74,526	96,965	150,167	180,794	216,638
% ROC		1.79%	5.17%	10.35%	16.36%	23.34%	31.45%	40.93%	63.39%	76.32%	91.46%
REVERSION SALES PRICE			6,333,807	7,015,255	7,805,604	8,724,045	9,763,207	11,039,784	12,495,259	14,196,769	16,188,121
COST OF SALE (5%)			316,690	350,763	390,280	436,202	489,660	551,989	624,763	709,838	809,406
ASSET MGMT. FEE (1%)			63,338	70,153	78,056	87,240	97,932	110,398	124,953	141,968	161,881
1st LOAN BALANCE		4,549,460	4,459,654	4,362,256	4,259,923	4,151,289	4,035,966	3,913,543	3,783,581	3,645,618	3,499,160
MEX LOAN BALANCE		569,812	466,108	356,020	239,153	115,090	(16,611)	(156,422)	(304,841)	(462,398)	(629,657)
PROCEEDS AVAILABLE		-	1,029,016	1,876,063	2,838,192	3,934,222	5,186,260	6,620,276	8,266,803	10,161,743	12,347,331
Commerce		950,000	1,500,851	2,270,553	3,147,378	4,149,008	5,296,221	6,613,442	8,129,394	9,877,665	2,469,466
Q-II, Plus		79,016	375,213	567,638	786,844	1,037,252	1,324,055	1,653,361	2,032,349		
NET C-F + S/R + REV.		1,090,301	1,998,678	3,031,938	4,210,629	5,558,890	7,105,099	9,017,637	11,065,713	13,430,523	

Conclusion

That is some of my journey into this business. It is still unfolding. I have the $60,000,000 game we are playing, but it is the journey where the juice is, not getting to the end goal. Once there, another game has to be played so that the journey continues.

The goal of this book is to show you that if I can get into this game and play, so can you. As anyone who knows me or our core group will tell you, there is absolutely nothing special about us. We do not have any special gene. If a guy like me can get into the world of self-storage and play at the level at which we are currently playing, anyone can. You do not have to have money, connections, or some special trait to win at this game. I would say to win you need a desire to play. Not just a hope or wish, but a desire that burns deep—so deep that a crystal-clear goal is there. A goal that causes you to organize your life around it.

Then you need some special knowledge. Self-storage is an operating business and a real estate play together. This book and other resources out there will give you all the knowledge you need. Keep an eye on **www.CreatingWealthThroughSelfStorage.com** for updated products and resources. Read the blogs and connect with the resources the site provides. And yes, the Valuator, or a tool like it, is essential so you know a project that fulfills your goal when you see it. That is what is required for you to play this game.

So what is your next move? What needs to happen where you are that gets you in the game, or takes you to the next level? If I can be a resource for you, do not hesitate to contact me at **www.CreatingWealthThroughSelfStorage.com**.

Made in the USA
San Bernardino, CA
15 February 2019